The Spirit of Teams

UXBRIDGE COLLEGE
LEARNING CENTRE

The Crowood Press

First published in 1999 by
The Crowood Press Ltd
Ramsbury, Marlborough
Wiltshire SN8 2HR

British Library Cataloguing-in-Publication Data
A catalogue record for this book is available from the British Library.

ISBN 1 86126 051 2

Typeset by Phoenix Typesetting, Ilkley, West Yorkshire
Printed and bound in Great Britain by
WBC Book Manufacturers, Mid Glamorgan

Contents

Acknowledgements

When a book is compiled from personal experience it is almost impossible to acknowledge properly all the people who must have contributed to the author's learning. From Stan Jones at Barton Primary school, who organized and inspired perhaps his most successful under-ten soccer team ever in 1958–59, through my time with many coaches and managers in hockey, to the senior business leaders with whom I am now privileged to work, my thanks for your contribution to my understanding.

In particular I wish to acknowledge the following: Roger Self, OBE (Great Britain Men's Hockey Team Manager 1984 and 1988 Olympics) with whom I worked for eight years with the team during the 1980s. His great experience, unique style and his total support and trust in my coaching offered me great learning opportunities. Together we explored new territory in developing high-performing teams.

Bernie Cotton (Great Britain Men's Hockey Team Management 1988 and 1992 Olympics), who probably had to deal with more of my team development ideas and conversations than anyone else during our association of eleven years in international performance. His ability to help me clarify my thoughts assisted immeasurably.

Susan Slocombe, OBE (Great Britain Women's Hockey Coach, Atlanta Olympics 1996) has immense experience in the practical application of the principles and processes of team development in the international arena. Her rigorous approach to the testing of every concept and to finding specific practical examples for every aspect of team development explored within this book has kept it grounded in reality and, in doing so, enhanced it greatly.

David Hemery, MBE and Sir John Whitmore are my two business partners who have helped me to explore the core elements of high quality coaching during our fifteen-years association. They have been inspirational.

Ken Hathaway at The Crowood Press, whose patience and confidence have been both remarkable and enormously valued.

Rosemary Philcox, who, in a masochistic moment, agreed to convert my scribbles into English and has managed to continue to do so despite the ebb and flow of my output.

Finally, my two sons Kester and Alexander, who, although now adult, accepted my absences during their childhood while I was away developing teams. To them I add my love to my thanks.

Preface

This book is about human beings and how they combine their energies to produce high-quality teamwork and high performance. It is not a blueprint for excellence, for there is none in the arena of team performance. My objective is to offer some of my accumulated experience of working with teams to enable you to become even better than you are at present.

If the thoughts and questions assist you to learn more about yourself and your team, to consider new or better ways in which you might promote teamwork of higher quality within your team, and to establish new ways forward for yourself and your team, then I shall have achieved my objective.

Understanding and promoting high-quality teamwork is recognized as one of the key qualities of the best coaches. Today, the high achievement of teams is the result of the combination of technique, fitness to perform, tactics and teamwork, with the quality of the last becoming a major factor differentiating the best from the rest.

This book makes no apology for looking in detail at the way in which teams develop and work together, for it is the process of choosing to work co-operatively and continually seeking to improve the level of co-operation that generates the almost indefinable 'spirit' of successful teams.

As sport becomes more professional in both its structures and processes there will be an even greater need for more people not only to understand team development but also to be able to promote team growth actively.

As the business world continues to advance, the critical, competitive edge has become the people in it and the quality of their teamwork. Businesses now need new entrants who recognize and value the importance of both team working and team performance. This means that these should be important elements in the education of our young people.

While this book is written from experiences in the performance of elite teams, I believe that the principles and processes in that world are applicable to all teams at all levels and in every walk of life.

Introduction

Between 1980 and 1988 I was privileged to be the coach to both the England and the Great Britain men's hockey teams. During that time we achieved something I shall always treasure: 'we became the best we could be'.

I was not alone in the process. Roger Self, Colin Whalley and Bernie Cotton were team managers at various times who offered differing and yet important strengths. Physiologists, doctors (Stephen Thomas and Peter Verow), physiotherapists (Barry Maddox and Kevin Murphy) and assistant coaches (John Hurst, Mike Hamilton, Keith Sorrell and Richard de Figuerado) all contributed greatly to the management teams during this time. Above all, however, there were the players. A group of about forty men who were committed to achieve the highest standards possible, given the constraints of being amateur players with full-time jobs, some having families and all suffering from limited funding, scarce facilities and competing nations who valued elite performance more highly than Britain.

The combination was powerful. The leadership of the management teams was continually focused on high performance and the players responded positively to this challenge. The culture within the squads shifted away from prescribe and control towards acknowledge, create and empower, away from directive team management towards partnership agreements.

The results of these developments were evident at two levels. We won more matches and more medals than ever before in a decade (Olympic Bronze, European and World Silver and Olympic Gold). We caused a group of performers to accelerate away from the remainder of the sport in Britain, not only in their personal standards but also, and probably more importantly, in their teamwork.

They became the best they could be and this enabled them to accomplish the results. Within this 'best they could be' I would include the qualities technically, tactically, physiologically and psychologically.

In my opinion the best tournament we played was not the Seoul Olympics but in Moscow a year earlier (1987) at the European Cup, even though we lost the final to the Netherlands (on penalty flicks). It was during this tournament that we experienced domination over every opposing team. To achieve this but lose the final was both painful and exhilarating, yet a powerful learning experience too.

The most effective tournament performance was, of course, at the Olympic Games in Seoul and it is for this that the team will always be remembered. We were not, as many people think, outsiders who won gold against the odds. By 1988 we were ranked second in the world and had to reach the final to justify our ranking. Never before had any team from Britain been rated so highly before the tournament! Achieving one place higher than our ranking was a testament to the skill, belief and commitment of all involved and the way they worked together.

The thoughts of a player in a letter to me after the Olympics captured the whole essence of a high-performing team: 'I was encouraged/allowed to play the way I most enjoyed and which could offer most to the team. We were an incredibly strong team without losing the individual talents of each player.' I read those words and feel proud to be part of a management which helped to generate that culture.

If this book can assist you in your progress towards promoting exceptional team performance then I shall have achieved my purpose. I cannot give you a magic answer or quick-fix solution for there are none. I can only offer you my experiences (both unsuccessful and successful) and my thoughts gathered along the way.

In my desire to help you to become even better than you now are I would like to:

- offer you practical ideas
- challenge your thinking
- challenge my own thoughts
- help you to reflect on your interaction with performers
- immerse you in team concepts.

None of this is done to try to show you a particular way of doing things for there is no 'right' way of developing exceptional team performance. It is my wish to help you to add whatever you personally need to become the best team coach you can be.

CHAPTER ONE

Team Spirit – What Is It?

'Team spirit is something you get just after you have won.'

This cynical view of team spirit was given by a soccer manager and, of course, there is an element of truth in the statement in that after success the team spirit is very evident. However, that is not to say it was neither there before the success nor central to its achievement.

Team spirit is not always easy to see but without it the team cannot grow. So what is it? A simple dictionary definition is: 'the willingness to act as a member of a group rather than an individual'. While this captures the essence of the team, I feel that it needs a little clarification if we are to use it as a basis for our understanding of what we are trying to promote in teams.

Willingness is clearly about choosing to do something. Choice can only be done effectively at the individual level. Even a team decision will require every individual to choose personally to follow that decision, otherwise it will not work as well as it might. When we choose to do something we are taking ownership and responsibility for our behaviour. Inherent in this choice is the acceptance of accountability for our actions.

Team leaders or developers are searching to work with people to unlock that willingness and desire to work co-operatively.

Individual versus Team

'If you want an exceptional team, keep your eye on the individual.'

One of the fundamental paradoxes in developing high-quality team performance lies within this simple yet challenging statement. And yet there are other well-known expressions regarding teams that appear to run counter to it, including: 'there is no "I" in team' and 'the team is more important than the individual'.

These are well-meaning strap lines that focus our attention on the need for the individual to be willing to integrate his or her personal goals, attitudes and behaviour with those of the team. They are evidently true in high-performing teams, but they are not so relevant in promoting teamwork in a newly-formed team.

The fact is that teams are made up of individuals and any team improvement has to be accepted or agreed to by each member at the individual level if the team is to receive the maximum return on that aspect of change. The truth is that individuals are important in teams and their willingness to adapt their behaviour to enhance team performance is critical. When everyone willingly is commited to changes designed to improve performance the effect can be startling.

It is then that we can feel 'the whole being greater than the sum of its parts'. It is then that we behave in a way that illustrates 'no "I" in team' or 'the team is more important than the individual'. (In truth, I prefer 'the team and the individuals are equally important'.)

However, the achievements which resulted in these feelings and behaviour were based upon individuals' choosing to work co-operatively. Helping performers to choose to make changes is a fundamentally important part in building exceptional teams. The best tactics in the world will not work unless they are skilfully implemented by committed performers.

Throughout this book I encourage the reader to keep both the individual and the team (or sub-team) in focus. I cannot see that teams are anything other than individuals, committed to agreed common goals, who choose to work together in ways which utilize their strengths and enable the whole to achieve much more than would otherwise have been possible.

Teams thrive on individual choice and commitment. In sport and in life the most powerful teams are made up of individuals who have chosen to work as a team.

CHAPTER TWO

What Makes a Team?

What Is a Team?

Anyone involved with teams can quickly offer a workable and acceptable definition of the word 'team'. Take a moment to consider your definition and then write it down.

Most definitions include the words 'people', 'working together' and 'common goals'. So anything along the lines of : 'a number of people who choose to work together to achieve a common goal' is acceptable. But is it enough?

Team or Group

Few would disagree that this is a reasonable definition of the word. But is it sufficient? Does it help us to differentiate between groups and real teams?

A business *committee* certainly agrees to work together and one assumes that it has a common goal. But is it a team? The people on the committee may come from several departments and the whole purpose of their inter-action may be to represent specific views and report on activities, progress, achievements and future plans. These all seem important and yet there may be little need to hear the views of other members of the committee on how they achieve these things, as it is work they perform independently and for which they are solely accountable. Not much sense of a team in this instance and, of course, in this example the committee are working more as a *group*.

However, when the same committee has to prepare a co-ordinated strategic plan for their organization or their part of it then things change. Now they are having to produce something together, will need continuing liaison and agreements between themselves, and will all be held account-able for its quality, effectiveness and even implementation. Now this activity will be quite different from the previous one.

There is nothing wrong with being a group. The key thing is to recog-nize when you need to be a team and when you are a group.

Real Teams

In defining real teams some amplification of the simple definition of 'team' is required. Real teams:

- recognize the power of having a small number of people in teams or sub-teams
- establish 'performance goals' which underpin, support and act as stepping stones to the common objectives
- generate real work or outputs together that could not be generated by the individual team members (focus upon 'interdependence')
- establish ways of working together that promote and support high levels of co-operation
- establish high levels of mutual accountability.

First, it appears inappropriate just to say 'a number of people'. What number? Any number? Can we have an effective team of twenty, forty or eighty? This clearly depends on what we mean by effective. A large number of people could have a common goal but it would probably have to be pretty vague in order to have general agreement. They could also agree on some ways of working together, although these are likely to be principles rather than specific behaviour or actions. All-in-all, effective teams tend to be small in the number of their members. It is no surprise that in sports with larger teams in which interdependence is high (soccer, hockey and rugby) there are accepted sub-teams whose teamworking within the whole is important. Initially 'forwards' and 'backs' were expressions of this but now many more subtle variations exist. In fact, teams in these sports could be seen nowadays as made up of players who have continually to form and reform into small teams during play: a whole series of fast-forming teams. But more of that later.

Even though a common goal is powerful in that it provides a clear focus for a team, that in itself may be insufficient to generate high-quality teamwork. Setting the winning of a championship (or even a game) as a common goal is highly motivating yet not totally within the control of the people who set it. And if it is not totally within their control then other goals which are have to be set. The performers do not have complete control over everything relating to winning the 4 x 100m relay race and, in particular, as regards the other competitors. In this case the goal of winning is still valid and motivating, but the focus needs to be on achieving things that are within the performer's control and may lead to success if he gets them right (such as his performance, the change-overs, tactics, pre-race preparation and mental rehearsal). These 'performance goals' help to turn the common goal into personal goals (behaviour or actions) over which the team members have much greater control. The best teams recognize the imperatives of performance goals and continually set, monitor and review them. They are also, of course, one of the key methods of evaluating changes in performance.

Establishing and promoting the key working principles and practices which the team members agree to adhere to in their teamworking is perhaps the most challenging and important area for both performers and management. This work is at the core of every high-performance team. It includes principles and practices related not only to teamwork during performance but also to areas such as behaviour outside of performance managing internal competition and conflict, generating feedback and communication issues. It is essential for any team that aspires to high performance to explore this area and to assess itself and its members continually against the agreed criteria. These agreed ways of working together are at the heart of teamwork and team spirit.

The final area identified in the best teams and which enhances the definition is 'mutual accountability'. This is where all the members of the team accept that they are jointly and together responsible and answerable for their performances.

In the best teams all members hold themselves accountable for all their joint agreements. They illustrate this mutual accountability through their behaviour and actions, that is, in the way they work with one another. Team members choose to accept mutual accountability and this ownership or responsibility is generated through the way the team and its teamwork are developed by the coach/manager.

It is on the generation of ways of working co-operatively and the promotion of mutual accountability that this book is focused.

A more complete definition of 'team' comes from Katzenbach and Smith in their book on business teams, *The Wisdom of Teams*: 'A relatively small number of people with complimentary skills committed to a common purpose, performance goals and ways of working together for which they hold themselves mutually accountable.'

In addition to being a definition it is possible to use the elements of this to measure progress or identify where energy needs to be focused to help in building the foundations for the team.

Focus your attention upon your team (this may be the playing team or the management team): consider the team against the criteria in Table 1. Give the team a 1 to 10 score (10 high) and make any notes for yourself that come out of this reflection, such as areas to work on or pieces that are missing.

This snapshot of your team as seen by you may, in itself, highlight some aspects that could benefit from closer attention and development. These observations could be enhanced still further were the views of others, including the team members themselves, solicited.

The mere process of collecting the views and discussing the findings

Question	Response (1–10)	Key Learning Points
Is there a strong fit of complementary skills within the team?		
Is there an agreed common purpose of the team?		
Have key performance goals been agreed at individual, sub-team and whole-team levels?		
Have the key 'ways of working' been identified and agreed?		
What is the level of mutual accountability for team process and performance?		

Table 1. Team Assessment

would probably open up avenues of action that enhance the teamworking and positively influence the ratings.

Understand More about Your Teamwork

Teams may differ dramatically. Not only do different sports demand differing kinds of teamwork, but there are also great differences between two teams in the same sport. The former is a function of the level and focus of the interdependency within the team, whereas the latter is related much more to the quality of the teamwork and the variety of abilities of the individuals who make up the team. This section is about the first of these two areas – the level and the focus of the interdependence within a team.

It is clear that teams differ in the way they work. A squash team differs from a rowing team, which differs from a netball team, which differs from a basketball team, and so on. But how do they differ, and how will an increased understanding of the differences enhance our ability to develop our own teams?

There are some obvious differences of size and activity, but one of the critical yet often overlooked differences relates to the interdependence between the team members. For example, in a squash team there is no real interaction between team members, whereas in rowing it is high and highly prescribed. In basketball, soccer and hockey it is high throughout the performance and dynamic, whereas in cricket and netball it varies considerably.

Interdependence is the *sine qua non* for teamwork. It is important to identify in which situations and between which performers the team needs the greatest interdependence in order to maximize its performance, and then what is required from each participant during them.

Two questions may help team coaches in this regard:

- which team members interact most often with one another and therefore need to work most effectively with one another?
- in which situations could the sub-team illustrate higher quality teamwork to the benefit of performance?

The answers to these may identify the areas on which to focus attention and energy since it is the enhancement of these that will probably bring the greatest improvement.

Having said this, it is vital to retain a balance between team and individual expression since both are important. It is no surprise nor coincidence that teams made up of individual performers (as in squash, gymnastics or tennis) often emphasize 'teamness' around the real performance (the uniform, being seen together, support, praise, for instance), whereas teams which perform together (such as soccer, basketball or rugby) allow individualism to occur away from the pitch or court. There is no right or wrong way in this, only the critical importance of balance.

What is the balance within your teams? If one is lacking in some regard, how might you improve the situation?

What are the effects of this imbalance on:

- the individual performer(s)?
- the team?
- the performance?

How Many Teams Do You Have?

The truth is that you probably have more than you might think. Within my own sport (hockey) during my time as a national team coach, I noticed that we had, in addition to the playing team, also:

- a management team
- a selection team
- a performance development team (coached)
- a sports science team, and
- a medical team.

But our overall purpose was the same: to produce teams that could compete for medals at European, World and Olympic level.

Beneath this, the performance goals and the way they worked together differed between each team. These were established by exploring and agreeing on:

- the roles and responsibilities of each team member
- the personal goals of each team member
- the way the team members needed to interact in order to achieve the objectives and fulfil their personal and team responsibilities.

These points in themselves make an excellent agenda for a team meeting in the early life of these teams. The outcomes will help the team to move forwards positively and the process will provide the opportunity for team interaction and relationships to grow.

What Is the Real Goal for Team Coaches?

I would not want to devalue challenging goals such as 'winning a gold medal' or becoming the 'champion team' because they act as great motivators. This may, of course, be a critical part of the common purpose or objective of the team. However, it is the means to that end that are at the heart of the development of teams.

The 'spirit of teams' is the promotion of the willingness to work together rather than as individuals, for people to see and feel the gains from the whole being greater than the sum of its parts. And who else is going to generate this other than the coach and the management team?

The reality for the best coaches and teams is that:

- we are continually challenging ourselves and our performers to review and reset the criteria for high performance as we progress
- we recognize that the 'edge' is more often found within and is drawn from the performer through interaction with the coach.

It is therefore the quality of the process of working with performers which often distinguishes teams which achieve the challenging goals they have set themselves.

If the generation of the willingness to work co-operatively is imperative then we have to enable performers to focus upon both achievement and the way they work together; and to achieve this, we as the developers of teams, must do the same.

The challenge of promoting performance improvement has no finishing line, for both coach and performer must continually strive for ways of being even better. However, within this challenge there may be many specific performance targets which are clearly measurable and act as finishing lines of particular stages of the journey.

The core of this book focuses upon the processes that can be used to generate high-quality co-operation within teams and fuel the spirit of achievement.

CHAPTER THREE

Performance: a Race with No Finishing Line

What Is Winning?

Anyone who has coached or led a team will be aware that, however good the performance, there are always areas which can be developed to generate improvement.

The very best individuals and teams are continually seeking the 'edge' which will enable them to do things even better than before. In sport this may or may not lead to their 'winning' medals, championships or series. I doubt that a team or team management would choose not to work to promote improvements if they were informed that they would not win the championship. So what drives them to seek exceptional performance if winning is not guaranteed?

First, the definition of 'winning' is important. If the only 'win' is to beat others then there is going to be a great deal of disappointment along with the potential discouragement that may accompany it. And, of course, without any 'wins' over our competitors, interest and motivation may wane. Clearly motivating people and teams to improve performance is no straightforward matter. If it were simple we would have it cracked by now.

This is not to say that the goal of winning is not important as a motivator, it is just that it cannot be the only one, otherwise some individuals and teams would never start the journey.

Where Does It End?

What happens when we do win, be it at a micro level (a match) or a macro level (a championship or tournament)? Do we sit back and say, 'OK, that's the way we perform for the next year or two'? No, of course not. We immerse ourselves in reviewing our performance so that we can take it further in some way. This might be to do it better, or sooner in the contest, or for longer periods, or with great intensity, speed or effectiveness, or against even stronger and different opponents. We are rapidly dissatisfied with that level of performance. We recognize that others will soon replicate what we have achieved or go beyond it. There is a strong, natural drive within the human to improve. It does not take long for the outstanding performance to become the minimal expectation. Within this lies as many dangers as advantages.

Consider an area of team improvement: where the exceptional performance has rapidly moved towards the minimum expected. What have been the gains from this? What have been the negatives? How effectively did you handle this transition? What did you do that you were pleased with? What would you do differently in the future? What has been your key learning?

If we look at other fields such as music, dance or theatre in which performance is clearly evident and yet the competitive form of 'winning' is not so overt as in sport, we still find the striving for performance improvement at the forefront of the work. The musician and tutor or coach work to find ways of playing or interpreting the music ever more effectively. While this is obvious and causes no surprise, there is a subtle message here for those of us engaged in the development of teams.

The real focus of our work with teams needs to be on how we promote continuous performance improvement rather than on just trying to get to some kind of goal of 'winning'. In a way, this approach sits behind the cliché, 'take one game at a time'.

The reasons for this focus are simple:

- We may not yet know the details of the performance we shall need to achieve a 'win', it will need to be developed as we progress. In a tournament we prepare for the next challenge, while in a match we may modify the tactics. In both cases we recognize the on-going learning involved in the process of team performance.
- Performance improvement as we approach the edge of our current abilities or understanding is best made in small steps. Improvement comes from stretching beyond our current performance into a zone of risk and discomfort. Stretch too far and discomfort becomes great enough to inhibit performance. Make haste in small steps.
- Many of the improvements which culminate in outstanding performance come from the performers themselves. There is probably more self-correction and self-development during performance by the performer himself than many coaches would care to acknowledge. There is a great talent within the performer. Our role is to enable him or her both to develop these talents and to call upon them. The key to successfully achieving these objectives is the quality of the interactive process between coach and performer.
- Performance improvement is about learning and risk-taking, and to promote these successfully the performer has to be at the centre

of the process and we have to respond to his needs within the situation.

It's Not Just What You Do, It's the Way that You Do It

My experience continually reminds me that in the field of promoting human achievement we, the coaches, are core enablers, yet ultimately the performance and the achievement belong primarily to the performers. You will know what you have done to enable them to have the opportunity to be the best they are capable of at this given time and it will be the same whether they 'win' or not.

It is the way in which we work with people which is the core of our work. The ultimate achievements which spring from that working relationship are important yet different.

The way we work with people begins with ourselves. We have choice in the way that we view people. How often have you looked closely at the way you view people and compared it with the way in which you wish to be viewed by others?

For example, within your working relationship with your team to what extent do you:

- communicate 'winning' as achieving only the end result?
- give more energy to those who, in your view, are successful or winners?
- reward only winning?
- only set goals such as beating others or achieving the end result?
- feel that you hold the answers to success?

This is not judgmental, but merely raises our awareness of how we work with others.

Performance Is Not Potential

Reflect on your working role and consider these questions:

- What percentage of your potential within your working role has yet to be tapped?
- In which areas have you more which could still be utilized?

The actual percentage of your potential which you feel is as yet untapped is not particularly important. The key point is that you probably see yourself as having much more within you than has as yet been used. I have no doubt that you could take this further by looking at the evidence that you have for the belief that there is more potential within you, and also at the factors which you believe may be holding back the realization of this potential in performance.

I wonder what the performers in your team or squad might answer if they were asked the same questions. I have no doubt that they too would see themselves as having more within them than had been hitherto tapped into.

If we take ourselves a little further along this path, it is not long before we realize that, while we are willing to believe that there is unexploited potential within ourselves, we are less willing to demonstrate that belief in the way we work with others. How often do we so easily and quickly confuse a person's performance with his potential? If, however, I were to suggest that your present performance in any particular area was also your potential, then I believe that you might wish to have a serious conversation with me. The truth of the situation would be that you would see more within yourself than had as yet shown itself in performance.

Do we as humans have a unique weakness that we are incapable of seeing the potential in other people? We know that the answer to this is in the negative because we spend many years choosing to see the potential in our children even when they have done little to justify that belief in their future abilities. So what is going on in these situations? It is probably something to do with the fact that with our children we are continually choosing to seek positive evidence of their abilities or their potential, whereas all too often in other situations we choose or feel forced to look for the negative aspects of performance.

There is some key learning for us as developers of peak performance both in ourselves and in others from these examples. First, performance and potential are different and our performance is not a simple window on to our potential. The potential within a human being is a rich, complex mixture of knowledge, skills, experience and attitude of mind. Secondly, converting potential into performance has as much to do with the acknowledgement of the potential as with reviewing the current performance. The interactive process with the performer is as important as the content of the interaction. This is relevant for both the individual who is seeking to improve his or her own performance as well as for the coach or manager who is seeking to develop that of others.

Our willingness to see the potential in others does not guarantee success, but seeing people as unable to achieve things – as having little potential for improvement, in other words – probably does guarantee disappointment. To visualize myself doing something extremely well does not mean that I shall automatically succeed in it, but to see myself doing it badly probably does mean that I shall have a poor performance.

Let us explore further how people may view 'performance'. When did you last surprise yourself in some aspect of your own performance?

Perhaps you completed a course of physical activity which was especially challenging, or handled a particular business situation more expertly and than you thought yourself capable of, or made a presentation more successfully than you expected, or achieved something more easily than you thought possible, or sustained the quality of your performance for longer than you had previously managed to do. The specific situation in which you experienced these feelings may have been work or your hobby or a sporting activity. The environment in which it occurs is irrelevant because the principles and processes which underpin what is happening in these situations is common to all environments.

When these things occur we often say of the performance or of ourselves things such as 'I didn't realize that I had it within me to do that.' In fact, sometimes we are so amazed by what we have achieved that we devalue both the achievement and the process by saying things such as 'beginner's luck'! The fact remains that, because you achieved it, you did have it within you and if you had full control over all the aspects of the performance it was probably not beginner's luck nor simply lucky.

Let me offer an example. Occasionally while sitting at a desk we may be making notes on a piece of paper and suddenly realize that what we are writing is inappropriate. We may screw up the paper and, still with a pencil in our dominant hand, look for the wastepaper basket, holding the screwed-up paper in our other hand. On seeing the basket a few metres away in the corner of the room, we throw the paper with our non-dominant hand and it lands miraculously in the basket. We sit for a few seconds amazed at our achievement and then perhaps begin to analyse it and try and decide what we did to make it happen. We then screw up some more pieces of paper and, by positioning our non-dominant hand, elbow and arm in a number of places and aiming in various ways, attempt to repeat the performance, but sadly without much success. Then, being unable to analyse it to our satisfaction and repeat the success, we label the first throw as lucky or beginner's luck. The reality, of course, is quite the opposite. The first attempt which went straight into the basket probably more closely reflected our true ability. We had full control over the whole action and performed it smoothly and naturally. There was no sudden wind nor assistance from any outside force to help us to succeed. It was probably a combination of our over-analysis of our technique plus our trying too hard to repeat it, and a little voice reminding us that it was unlikely that we could repeat that success twice or three times in a row that led to our subsequent, disappointing performances. There were some complex forces at play in the performance, some of which we do not fully understand as yet, but the purpose of this example is to illustrate the power that mind has in the performance arena.

There are many examples in all aspects of life where people have achieved high performance and, while realizing that their knowledge, skill, experience and fitness were important, recognised that the critical factors had much more to do with what was going on in their mind both before and during the performance. Our actions and our results are therefore greatly influenced by what is going on in our minds. Achieving peak performance is therefore largely about enabling people to become aware of what goes on to influence their state of mind. This is important for not only promoting my personal performance but also in generating high performance by others. I need to understand how I may best interact both with myself for my personal performance and with others to promote their performance.

If I say 'I cannot get the players nowadays', then I probably never shall find players of the appropriate standard. The reality will be that I shall probably see only the evidence which confirms and reinforces my initial view. If in the area of personal improvement I say to myself 'I cannot see myself doing that', what chance might I have of getting halfway there?

The combination of the value others demonstrate to us and the value we give to ourselves is particularly powerful and important in the conversion of potential into higher performance.

In our drive towards peak performance one of our principle challenges is to understand more clearly the kind of interaction with ourself and with others that is most likely to unlock the potential and convert it into performance. While coaches can contribute much to the performer, the greatness of their performance lies within him or her alone. The challenge for team coaches is to work with both the individuals and the team to unlock potential and cause it to be converted into performance.

If we recognize that the mind is key, then we need to understand the key to the mind.

Belief, Value and Will

One way of beginning to understand what we need to promote within an individual and in teams to generate improved performance is to recognize the processes a person goes through which enables him to take on a new challenge. This is a much more positive approach in promoting improved performance than the focusing upon all the hurdles that have to be overcome and the difficulties that one could face.

Reflect for a few moments upon the latest challenge, whether it be a project, a task or a promotion that you have accepted in your working life. What caused you to accept the offer? What did you see in yourself that gave you the feeling that you could succeed? Your answers to these questions will be right for you and, while they may not fit the simple process I am going to outline, they will, I hope, serve to illustrate clearly what generally happens within a human being with regard to the improvement of performance.

Experience suggests that there are three important elements for someone to explore when he is seeking to improve performance; these are:

- believing he can do it
- seeing the value in it, and
- being willing to try.

At first sight these appear obvious but, if we are willing to look into them a little closer, we actually find that they are key stepping stones to the improvement of performance in almost any field.

Belief that I Can Do It

Belief in our own ability to achieve is a cornerstone of success and, while we recognize its importance, it is only when we explore it more deeply that we can find the factors that underpin our belief and enable it to grow.

The question, 'What did you see within yourself that enabled you to believe that you could do it?' often uncovers the factors which underpin belief. These include knowledge, experience, skills, competences and attitudes. All these may have a direct affect, both positive or negative, upon our belief that we can improve matters in any area of performance. The more these factors are positively aligned and supportive of one another, the greater will be the self-belief.

While, as a developer of a person, I may struggle to influence in a direct manner his belief that he can improve performance, I most certainly can have a positive effect indirectly through the exploration of the factors which underpin his belief.

I can assist someone to investigate the experience, knowledge, skills and competences that he has and relate them to the challenges of the area identified for performance improvement. I can enable him to see what he has to contribute and what he may need to develop in order to promote an improvement in performance. I can help him to gather the evidence, or challenge his perceptions, in order to elicit as clear a picture as possible.

I can also help him to explore the attitudes he has towards the role or the performance improvement and how he might use them or even modify them to promote success. Through this process I can have a positive impact upon the person's belief that he can improve his performance. It does not guarantee success, but it may have a significant impact upon the likelihood of it.

'Really Wanting to' or 'Seeing the Value'

A person's really wanting to do something is based upon his seeing the value in making the change. If he cannot see the value in it for himself then his interest, motivation and commitment towards the improvement are going to be lower. When people are asked for the reasons why they accepted their most recent challenging opportunity their responses often include some of the following:

> 'It allowed me to keep a job.'
> 'It satisfied my ambition to take on more responsibility.'
> 'It offered me a greater challenge.'
> 'It gave me more status.'
> 'It gave me greater personal control over my activities.'
> 'It provided me with more opportunity for personal development.'
> 'It gave me more money.'
> 'I felt that it was a more fulfilling and meaningful role.'

All of these reactions illustrate the value that the individual saw in taking the promotion or accepting the new opportunity. They all satisfy important human needs and without this satisfaction the motivation of the person is adversely influenced. Assisting people to recognize or uncover the value that a performance improvement will have for them personally (and the team) is a key stepping stone. Helping people to see how a performance improvement can satisfy one or more things that are truly valuable to the individual and to team effectiveness is a central plank in continuous performance improvement.

'Willingness to Try'

Whenever we seek to improve performance we are, by definition, asking ourselves and others to step where they have never been before. Every performance improvement demands that we go a little further than we have ever been before. To do this we have to be willing to take risks and promote risk-taking. This is a challenging area, as everyone's approach to risk-taking and the ability to promote it varies. When promoting risk-taking in another or even in oneself it is essential to achieve the delicate balance between something being challenging and yet achieveable. If the challenge or the risk is too great then the fear of failure may be inhibiting. If, however, our support for the risk-taking is inadequate, then the performer will lose trust in the process and fewer risks will be taken. The coach who encourages risk-taking by someone only to blame him if the risk does not produce success will rapidly erode the trust between himself and the performer. However, if no risk is ever encouraged then progress will be slow.

These three areas interact with one another in a complex way, but the process of exploring them and isolating them from each other has helped me to understand the areas in which I work with a performer, no matter what the issue, if I really wish to enable him to improve his performance. They also offer me the opportunity to identify where the blockages may be within a person with regard to performance enhancement.

If, as a coach to a performer, I work with one such that he believes that he can succeed, see the value in what he is doing and is willing to try, then clearly I shall provide the opportunity. This is, in fact, a simple process of both delegation and empowerment as well as of performance improvement.

Coaching is empowering delegation. High-quality coaching allows the performers to take the power which in turn unlocks their performance. In reality, this is the only way in which we can help teams to achieve exceptional performance, because they are the only ones capable of achieving it. We as coaches can no longer achieve these standards and so doing it for them will not work. Nor can we necessarily tell them exactly how to do it as we may not ourselves know, because we have never done it like that ourselves.

Coaches work in a strange world characterized by:

- co-ordinating and developing the talents of other people
- converting theory into practice
- establishing core principles while promoting creativity and innovation
- having considerable power along with almost total impotence
- challenging performers to go physically where we ourselves have been only in imagination.

It is a world in which the coach is promoting on-going learning while not knowing what that learning might be. Exceptional performance demands that we take ourselves and our performers beyond the frontiers of our own experience. If we are not prepared to go there ourselves, albeit in our thinking rather than in our actions, then how can we provide the leadership our performers need?

CHAPTER FOUR

Coaching and the Spirit of Achievement

What is it that high-quality coaching does that generates the spirit in teams and individuals to aspire towards and achieve high performance?

I have attempted within this section to capture through a simple analogy the key aspects that form the fundamental principles of the relationship between the coach and the performers, both individual and team. For simplicity, the analogy is of the relationship between a performer and a coach, but it is equally applicable to a sub-team, a whole team or even a squad, albeit with some minor modifications.

My encouragement to the reader throughout is to relate continually the principles and the examples to your team in your sport.

The Performer

Let us begin with the performer or the team because that is where the performance improvement is going to take place and let us call the performer 'Charlie' – a woman on this occasion.

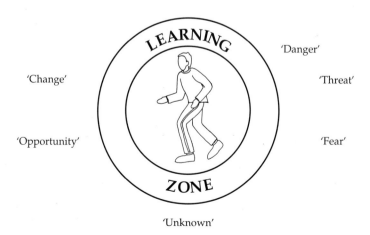

Fig. 1. Charlie Seeks to Improve Her Performance

Charlie has a level of competence or ability to which she performs comfortably at present. This zone might be called her zone of competence (or comfort) and is depicted in Figure 1 by a circle around her.

Outside this zone there is plenty of room for growth and expansion by Charlie and yet the willingness to stretch into it is often related to her view of this area. How do people view the area outside their zone of competence?

There are as many words to describe their views as there are views. A few are given in Figure 1. If the perception of the performer towards this area of potential growth is negative then the blockages to expansion will be even stronger than if their perception were more positive. However, the important point is that performance improvement requires an expansion of the zone of competence to include previously unexplored areas. For ease this area is called the 'zone of learning'.

Now how does the coach come into the relationship? Charlie's coach is on the outside, interacting with her to encourage and assist in the expansion of the zone of competence by stepping into the zone of learning.

This zone of learning also represents some of Charlie's as yet unfulfilled potential. We are not sure how much there is but it is almost certainly much larger than Charlie believes. There is too much evidence of people and teams achieving well beyond their own expectations and the expectations of others for us, as coaches, to dare to think otherwise. If you are uncertain of this ask yourself: 'What percentage of my potential has yet to be tapped into?' What is your gut feeling for this – 20 per cent, 50 per cent? It does not matter what the figure is, just notice that it is well above zero. And what if you asked your team what percentage of their potential has yet to be realized? What might they answer?

In addition, it must be remembered that Charlie's current performance is not a simple window upon her potential. Reflect on this since it is a fundamental principle if coaches are to generate the spirit of achievement in performers and teams.

Of course, the role of coach is to work with Charlie to address all the areas that will allow her to step willingly into the zone of learning and have the opportunity to achieve an improved performance. What does she need? When asked this question, performers and coaches have responded with words such as: support, recognition, safety, trust and trustworthiness, reasons, knowledge, incentives, self-belief, reward and 'OK to fail'.

If all of these are generated in the interaction between the coach and Charlie then there is every likelihood that she will successfully stretch into the zone of learning.

Unfortunately, one cannot predict in which direction that will be and, while we could always resort to fear and autocracy (that is to say, power) as the motive to shift Charlie in the direction we want, this provides only a short-term gain and is not ideal for on-going learning and performance improvement. The danger of this will be discussed in more detail later. Suffice it to say here that a culture of fear and autocracy does little to generate a positive spirit actively with teams and individuals. Some individuals may respond positively but that will be totally due to the performer and has not been actively helped by the coach.

All the needs of Charlie are therefore important to the coach and later chapters will expand upon how coaches may actively promote interactions that satisfy these needs and increase the willingness of performers, as individuals and teams, to expand their zone of competence and achieve high performance.

The Coach

Staying with the analogy of Charlie as the individual performer, or the team, I want to offer an overview of the areas in which the coach works to promote actively the spirit of high achievement within performers.

Coaches often see themselves as being able to influence only a relatively small part of the performance environment. I believe that coaches have a much greater influence and are able to foster a sophisticated relationship via a relatively simple process with the performer. This book seeks to explore and explain the principles and processes that underpin the relationship.

Earlier, the importance of potential was highlighted, for this is what Charlie is going to turn into reality (in skills and learning, for instance) as the zone of competence expands.

What is important for the coach is an awareness and understanding of the factors that inhibit potential from becoming reality, for these are the blockages to erode. They may be neatly split into two groups: internal and

Internal Blockages	External Blockages
Fear of failure	Lack of opportunity
Low confidence – 'I could not do that'	No risks taken
Low self-worth	Ideas not accepted
Previous negative experiences	Blame culture
	Autocratic style
	Poor listening

Table 2. Factors that Inhibit Our Potential from Becoming Reality

external. Some of these are shown in Table 2; check them and add any more that you have experienced.

As the coach, which of these two sets of blockages do you have the greatest control over? Of course, the external blockages are the things that you can do something about. And will you stop there? Can you afford to ignore the internal blockages, leaving the performer to deal with these and hoping that some good may result from your changes of the external factors? It is a choice that we have as a coach, but not one that is likely to promote the kind of spirit we seek.

The influence you can bring to bear upon the internal blockages will be the result of the quality of your coaching relationship – the 'how' in which you work with your performers.

Expectations, Potential and Achievement

The expectations coaches have of their performers and the expectations performers have of themselves can have a subtle yet powerful influence upon performance.

The way we view people has the power to influence the way in which we interact with them, which has the power to influence their performance. This effect is commonly known as the self-fulfilling prophecy and has been shown to occur in scientifically-designed studies related to human performance.

Understanding the potential effect of this is important to coaches in the creation of an environment and relationship to inspire achievement. Coaches who see their performers only as having low ability and unable to do things are probably setting up an environment and relationship that is going to result in under-achievement. There may be improvement but it is unlikely that the performers' true potential will be realized. In terms of the internal and the external blockages to potential, the coach probably adds to the internal factors through the emphasis upon the negative.

Although choosing to see the performers as able to achieve high performance does not guarantee success, it sets up a more positive environment and relationship, one more likely to erode external blockages to the realization of potential and to build a relationship that can assist in the release of the internal blockages. The erosion of these internal inhibitors encourages the spirit of 'I can'.

Sadly, performers do not need coaches to knock them down, they are quite capable of keeping themselves small. They see themselves as unable to achieve something or they account for success as 'lucky' or a 'fluke'. These are, of course, the internal blockages and are, in fact, manifestations of low expectation in the performer. The source of these low expectations is probably previous experience, and while in some cases it may be appropriate to understand the root cause in most situations, the most important issue is to promote higher self-worth and personal expectation.

During the thirty years I have been learning as a coach, I have found that performers – individuals and teams – follow a simple model when continually seeking performance improvement (exploring the learning zone). As described in Chapter Three, performers seek to improve when they:

- believe they can do it (knowledge, skills, abilities, attitude toward themselves and others)
- see the value in it (what they gain or how they benefit)
- are willing to try (how risk-taking is promoted and supported).

This is hardly profound, but it is true and is applicable to any learning situation. It illustrates the areas in which the coach works when interacting with performers to help them to stretch their zone of competence. It also provides a template that can assist the coach to identify where any blockages may exist.

If you refer to the list of needs that Charlie wanted to be fulfilled in order to step willingly into the zone of learning on page 35 and link these to the model above I am certain that you will see how they dovetail.

Motivation and Achievement

The final area that is central to the work of the coach is motivation or the generating of motives to act. This is considered in detail later, but it would be wrong to exclude from this overview such an important part of the coach's work in the coach–performer relationship.

Put simply, Charlie will be influenced by two sets of motivators: the intrinsic and the extrinsic. The former are those that are generated inside her while the latter are placed within her environment by others, and the coach in particular. Coaches have considerable control over extrinsic motivators but can influence the intrinsic only through the quality of their relationship with performers. It is the case that the intrinsic motivators are the stronger and the longer lasting, so that if we want to generate the spirit to aspire to the highest levels coaches must seek to access, generate and use the intrinsic motivation of performers.

Together Charlie and her coach seek to realize her potential. Neither can do it alone and the key is the relationship the coach generates.

The challenge for coaches is to establish a quality of interaction that is both honest and optimistic since this kind of relationship promotes and generates the attitudes that underpin a positive growth towards high achievement.

All too often in the past, team coaches have been wary of the relationship they have established with their performers. There has been a concern that closeness and understanding leads to a loss of power and effectiveness; as if it somehow erodes the leadership position of the coach. The reality, of course, is that all the great coaches have both understood and been very close to their performers. If they had not achieved both, they would never have engaged the performers at a sufficiently deep level to promote high performance. It is yet another paradox in coaching that one has to delve deep in order to go high!

A high-quality relationship between coach and performer does not preclude toughness, objectivity or high standards in the coach. The relationship is a partnership and partnerships have to be worked at if they are to achieve the highest returns. If the performers are important to you, then the relationship is worthy of close attention.

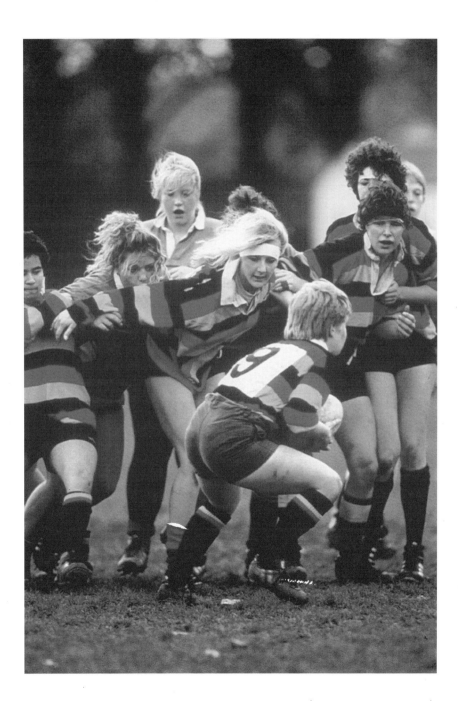

CHAPTER FIVE

Coaching Individuals and Team Performance

'Inner control leads to outer performance.'

It was not very long ago that performance was seen primarily as a function of technique and fitness. We believed that a concentration upon these two components would lead to improved performance, and, naturally, up to a point it did.

Then, as performers met with increasingly challenging opponents and targets this process failed to deliver the goods. The initial response was to assume that the more successful opponents were giving even more time to work on technique and fitness than ourselves, and we added more to our performers – without success. The more enlightened coaches stood back, thought and then suggested a different approach. What is stopping us from asking the performers who do achieve high standards about the key components that make up their success? The answers were obvious, with hindsight, yet extremely revealing. High achievers recognized that, while technique and fitness were of great importance, there was another, equally important component, the mind. Their state of mind – focus of attention, relaxed concentration, positive attitude – was critical to success.

This recognition by performers, coaches and the governing bodies opened the doors of sport to the psychologists, who now seem to be everywhere in the late 1990s. Many of them are doing excellent work in support

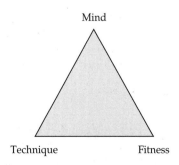

Fig. 2. Performance Components

of the performers and the coaches; others are failing to make the best of the opportunity (most probably due to poor communications and lack of agreement between themselves and the coaches): and some are potentially dangerous in the elevated status and importance they seek to carve out for themselves.

This recognition that performance has two key components: the body and the mind, opened up further understanding (see Figure 2).

Reflect on the number of occasions that individuals and teams with high-quality techniques and great fitness lose the contest. Now, we could put it all down to the failure of their technique and a less than total fitness, but that would be rather patronising to the underdog who in fact won. We could suggest that the underdog experienced a massive improvement in technique and fitness on that day; this is marginally possible and yet physiologically and biomechanically rather difficult to accept. So what is the reason for the result? The answer is often wrapped up in the words spoken by the successful underdog at the post-match interview:

There was little expected of us so we decided to go out and enjoy
    ourselves / go for it / show our critics they were wrong.
I/ We had nothing to lose.
I/we felt really well prepared and relaxed.
We were determined to sustain our focus throughout against such
    good opponents.

All these statements have everything to do with what is going on in the mind. This, in turn, can affect how technique and fitness are sustained and used, but the thoughts themselves cannot find any new technical abilities or fitness that are not there within the person.

The conclusion is entirely obvious. Much of the work of coaches is about helping performers to be clear in their minds, assisting them in their thought processes, for performance begins in the mind and it is the mind therefore that underpins and generates high performance.

The key challenges for me as a coach revolved around the questions:

- how can I best help the performers to gather and make use of all the information available both before and during performance?
- what state of mind do I need to generate to help them to maximize their opportunity to succeed?
- what do I have to do to help them to answer the key problems they face when I myself may not know all the solutions?

Fundamentally, coaching is about helping performers to learn, understand their collective knowledge and experience, recognize situations and apply their expertise to the achievement of successful outcomes.

Just as it was possible to establish that the 'mind' was a key component to high performance by investigating high performers, so greater insight can be gained about what the mind is doing so successfully by delving into what happens during this performance. In this way we may learn more about what we as coaches need to focus our attention upon in our work.

The High-performance Mind

High performance in almost any walk of life is the result of maintaining inner control over our outer actions. Without this control our actions may either run away with themselves or fail to match up to the needs of the situation. Interviews with performers give insights into this subtle and complex relationship between the inner and the outer world. People speak of their controlled aggression; their positive self-talk; that the game or the performance was 90 per cent in the mind; or perhaps of their ability to overcome doubts that they had about their ability to succeed. It is, of course, wrapped up in the much overused word 'focus' that we now hear so often from managers, coaches and performers.

What is it that the best performers are able to do? They seem capable of tuning their mind to gathering all the appropriate information at the right time (awareness) and then choosing the best response to the current situation (responsibility); the very best performers appear to be able to accomplish this under great pressure of time, speed, risk or a combination of all these. That people are able to do this there is no doubt. But are we able to develop this ability in ourselves and others – or do we have to accept that it is innate?

My belief is that, while all of us have innate abilities which are specifically ours, we all have the capacity to enhance these and through this achieve a performance improvement. The inner game is the ability to take in high-quality input from any situation, to use that and the accumulated learning from previous experiences, and then choose the best response to the situation. The more accomplished I am in this process, the more I am able, not only to achieve high performance at a particular moment, but also to apply the learning to future situations. Team coaching is about generating this ability in both individuals and teams. The process when described in this way sounds obvious and straightforward and yet it is challenging to sustain high performance. The reasons for this are related to factors such as:

- the speed at which the inputs have to be collected, processed and acted upon
- the complexity of the inputs facing the performer
- the power of interfering thoughts and inputs to disrupt performance.

If coaches can enable us to play the inner game well the result will be a much greater feeling of control over performance and performance improvement. This feeling of control has a positive impact upon the esteem that we give ourselves and self-esteem is one of the most powerful fuels for increased performance.

Coaching for High-performance – Generating Awareness and Responsibility

If inputs are so important to performance, how can we positively influence the quality of those that performers observe and take in?

Many people who have experienced high performance have attempted to describe what they noticed was happening during it. The truth is that their words can only rarely capture the exact feeling, but the words often illustrate that the human being has the capacity to absorb high-quality input in quantity. Performers speak of 'seeing things extremely clearly' or of 'actions appearing to take place more slowly' or that they felt 'cocooned within the situation and unaware of outside forces and pressures'. More specific statements have described details such as:

- 'feeling relaxed or well balanced'
- 'good rhythm'
- 'retaining concentration'
- 'seeing the ball very clearly'
- 'thinking clearly and positively throughout'
- 'taking ownership of my performance'
- 'making it happen'.

People who have experienced a traumatic situation such as a car crash often recount that everything appeared to be going in slow motion during those split seconds. Of course, time did not actually go more slowly then; those present on the occasion merely became highly aware of what was happening, manifesting a level of awareness far beyond that which was being applied before the situation came about (a lower level of awareness may even have been partly to blame for the accident). In many situations, had the persons been more aware of all that was happening they might even have been able to respond differently and avoided the occurrence. The hypothesis is therefore that if we can help people to gather high-quality information within any situation their opportunities to find the best responses to it are increased. This is exactly the process that is often used in advanced driving tuition when the driver is asked to comment on what he notices as he drives. As people describe what they are seeing and experiencing in more detail, their driving is enhanced.

They do not try to improve their driving, they are working on improving the quality of the relevant input. As they process this enhanced input, the outputs improve.

In the world of coaching, in both sport and business, we describe the gathering of high-quality, relevant information as 'awareness'. Our experience is that, as people become more aware within any situation, they have an increased opportunity to respond more effectively. They may be aware of what is happening around them (awareness) or what they are experiencing (self-awareness) or both.

Awareness is the product of focused attention, concentration and clarity. The *Concise Oxford Dictionary* defines aware as 'conscious, not ignorant, having knowledge', *Webster's Dictionary* adds 'aware implies having knowledge of something through alertness in observing or in interpreting what one sees, hears, feels, etc.', and *Collins English Dictionary* uses the words 'watchful, vigilant, wary, mindful and sensible'. Awareness is a valuable human ability, but frequently our general level of awareness is often poor. If we can raise our level of awareness, then we have the opportunity to gather inputs of much higher quality in any situation, rather as a microscope is used to help us to see details unobservable by the naked eye.

High performers have achieved this state of high awareness within their particular areas. It is specific to their sport and may be in what they see or hear or feel or a combination of all three. Awareness is an invisible ability available to us all of considerable depth. You and I may have the same quality of eyesight as a racing driver and yet he will see much more detail when driving than either of us. A conductor of an orchestra may have no better hearing than another person but he will hear so much more detail in the music.

Awareness has not been ignored by coaches but it has been misunderstood, undervalued and mistrusted. At best it has been seen merely as a useful addition to technique and fitness, something you might have but which is difficult to generate, something the performer should be responsible for creating or is there only in the 'natural' player. At worst, it has been viewed by coaches as a threat to their expertise, an enemy that could undermine their position and authority, and therefore something to oppose, ridicule and destroy.

Responsibility is the acceptance of the outcome of a course of action. Telling people to be responsible does not cause them to feel responsible for the outcome of their actions. In fact, when the instruction does not produce an improvement in performance they may:

- blame the coach because the advice came from that source, thereby holding him responsible
- blame themselves and lower their own self-perception of their ability to improve.

Neither response is productive because both are judgemental and fail to generate any real responsibility in the performer.

When performers accept, choose or take responsibility for their own thoughts and actions their performances will improve. This process is not promoted by instruction, it demands questions. Choosing to do something for the team generates a much greater commitment within the person but choice is denied by instruction.

This lack of trust in the power of 'awareness' and 'responsibility' has meant that we have been ignoring or failing to capitalize on a mental process or a state of mind that is central to performance enhancement. Awareness and responsibility are at least the equals of technique and fitness; both may be heightened or generated within the performer and this process is the responsibility of both the coach and the performers working in partnership.

The traditional approach to promoting high performance has been to instruct performers, to tell them of their awareness and their responsibility. This process denies and devalues the abilities, knowledge and understanding of the performer. It inhibits the development of awareness and responsibility and the performance improvements that can flow from this. Instruction generally denies choice and leaves power in the coach rather than generating power within the performer. Some performers are capable of tapping into their own awareness and choosing to take responsibility in spite of the autocratic style of their coach. But others are dominated and subordinate their personal awareness and responsibility to that of the coach. In both cases it is unlikely that the performers will realize their true potential.

Generating awareness and responsibility are central to the process of learning. They do not devalue technique or fitness, in fact they enhance and facilitate the development of technical and physical capabilities.

If there was only the right way of doing something, Dick Fosbury would never have flopped, the double-handed shots at tennis would never have appeared, ski jumpers would still keep the skis parallel in the air and many teams would play as they always did.

Performers have many of the solutions to performance improvement wrapped up within themselves. The nature of coaching is to acknowledge this, see performers in this light and interact in a way that taps into and enhances these talents. Generating awareness and responsibility accesses the inner abilities of performers, and questioning rather than instruction is the key to unlock awareness and responsibility. The process of asking effective questions also acknowledges the knowledge and experience of the performer and involves him deeply in his own learning. Instruction does neither.

The Power of the Question

The previous section focused on the importance of awareness and responsibility in promoting learning and performance improvement and emphasized that instruction was not an effective form of interaction in this process. To generate high levels of awareness and responsibility demands that we ask rather than tell, but not just any old question will do. We have to find the questions that have the effect of capturing attention and then of increasing awareness and responsibility.

The common approach in sport is to command the performers to 'watch the ball' or to 'focus on balance' or to 'relax'. Watching, focusing and relaxing may be the very actions that will enable the performer to improve or sustain performance, but the command does not cause it to happen. On the contrary, the instruction to relax may make the person more tense.

Let us look at several kinds of question and their likely effect in causing performers to be more aware of what they are doing or of what is happening. We shall use 'watching the ball' as an example from sport.

Are you watching the ball?

This usually produces a yes/no answer. It does not generate high-quality input because the answer is low on detail and may even be untrue. These 'closed questions' are useful for confirming information and detail but they fail to generate awareness in the performer. Closed questions always begin with a verb and are therefore easy to recognize and alter.

Why are you not watching the ball?

This type of question is seen as very powerful by coaches. Unfortunately, it almost always generates defensiveness in the performer that may lead to a closing down of his awareness and a lowering of self-confidence. Neither of these effects contributes to learning and improved performance.

How do you feel about your watching of the ball?

This kind of question is open rather than closed and avoids the inferred criticism of 'why', but tends to draw out responses such as 'OK' or 'fine'. These lack the detail and specificity so important in awareness. The reason is simple. The question is vague and so the response is likely to be vague too.

These are not every effective questions, but consider the effect of the following:

- What do you notice about the ball as it comes towards you?
- Which way is the ball spinning?

- How quickly is the ball spinning?
- What is the trajectory or path of the ball?

These questions are of a different nature because they generate different effects.

- in order to answer the question the performer is compelled to attend to the ball
- the performer has to focus more closely or to a higher level to provide the degree of accuracy demanded by the question
- the answers are descriptive rather than judgemental and this lowers the risk of self-criticism and of damage to self-esteem
- the higher-quality verbal responses from the performer provide an all-important feedback for the coach which offers the opportunity to verify the accuracy of the answers and therefore the quality of concentration.

Instruction and the less effective form of question do not achieve any of these effects. The result of using effective questions is that they generate in the performer high levels of awareness and offer the opportunity for the performer to produce improved responses. This process empowers the performer.

Is this not what coaches in sport are seeking? To enable the performer to take real responsibility for his or her performance so that in the competitive arena they (individuals or teams) have the capability to see what is really happening and to modify the performance accordingly. If this is so then let us put instruction where it truly belongs, as a small part of our interaction with performers. While learning and performance enhancement are important, the generating of awareness and responsibility is paramount.

This high-quality coaching interaction based upon the use of effective questions to generate awareness and responsibility has an important impact on the spirit of the team. The process generates the following positive effects:

- performers are truly involved in their own learning and development
- the knowledge and experience of the performer are both valued and utilized
- performers participate in the creation of their own future performance
- individuality and uniqueness are acknowledged and integrated rather than excluded
- empowerment is the natural outcome
- a clear focus upon performance enhancement, yet through the involvement of the performer

- performers who are more self-reliant, self-monitoring and self-motivated.

Regrettably, all too often these developments are seen by coaches as threats to their own positions. The reality is that they provide coaches and performers with the opportunity to work together at creating high levels of performance and teamwork.

GROW – the Sequence for Effective Questions

We have established that the art of promoting high-quality performance is all about focusing the mind of the performer through the use of effective questions. In addition, these questions need to be carefully constructed to have the desired effect of generating awareness and responsibility. Finally, there is a further subtlety in that the sequence of the questions is also important.

There are significant advantages if the effective questions cause the performers to become increasingly aware of:

- what they want to achieve → *goal*
- what is happening now → *reality*
- what they could do → *options*
- what they will do → *will*

The four words *goal, reality, options* and *will* yield the acronym GROW. Through this increased awareness the performers will explore and discover improved responses in themselves.

The Reasons for Having a Sequence

GROW provides a neat structure to the interaction between performer and coach. It transforms a pleasant conversation into a purposeful, highly focused and progressive interaction. The sequence ensures that all the main aspects related to a performance-improvement situation will be addressed rather than ignored, forgotten or passed over.

While the sequence may appear rather formal at first it actually provides structure to a natural progression thus strengthening rather than weakening the process.

It might be argued that many performance issues begin in *reality* from which the *goal* emerges. While this is partially true there is the danger of accepting this as normal. Exploring reality first is likely only to produce goals based upon the present reality, that is, they will address the immediate issue. This might treat a symptom rather than the real cause of the

Content / Structure	Focus of Performers Attention	Questions
Goal What do you want to achieve?	Clear picture of future success Positive Areas within control The value of achieving success	What is the aim of this discussion? What do you want to achieve long-term? What does success look like? How much personal control or influence do you have over your goal? What would be a milestone on the way? When do you want to achieve it by? Is that positive, challenging, attainable? How will you measure it?
Reality Where are you now?	Honest appraisal of present situation In depth detail More than one perspective Clear picture of gap between 'where we are' and goal	What is happening now? (What, when, where, how much, how often) Who is involved (directly and indirectly)? When things are going badly on this issue, what happens to you? What happens to others directly involved? What is the effect on others? What have you done about this so far? What results did that produce? What is holding you back from finding a way forward? What is really going on? (intuition)
Options What could you do?	Creativity Generate ideas Non-judgemental Challenge assumptions	What options do you have? What else could you do? What is . . . ? (time, power, money, etc.) Would you like another suggestion? Which options interest you most?
Will What will you do?	Action steps Commitment Tackle obstacles Support needed	Which option or options do you choose? To what extent does this meet all your objectives? What are your criteria and measurements for success? When precisely are you going to start and finish each action step? What could arise to hinder you in taking these steps? What personal resistance do you have, if any, to taking these steps? What will you do to eliminate these external and internal factors? Who needs to know what your plans are? What support do you need and from whom? What will you do to obtain that support and when? What could I do to support you? What commitment on a 1–10 scale do you have to taking these agreed actions? What prevents this from being a 10? What could you do or alter to raise your commitment closer to 10? Is there anything else you want to talk about now or are we finished?

Table 3. Performance and Focus

problem. Only by exploring *goal* in detail will a vision of future success emerge. If an issue begins in *reality* it is better to visit *goal* in detail as soon as possible if a step change in performance is required.

This simple structure is exactly that: a structure for the dialogue. It is not coaching. GROW is only as powerful as the context within which it is applied, and the most powerful context is that of awareness and responsibility. Coaching is the process of generating *awareness* and *responsibility* within the performers. The process is enhanced through the use of effective questions rather than instructions.

Table 3 offers a guide to the appropriate focus of attention required with each phase of GROW and some of the generic, effective questions that promote the required focus. Coaches will rapidly recognize that once the required focus of attention is understood there are many more questions that may be used over and above those offered as examples. The best questions will be those that are specific to the situation under consideration and those will be found only when the issue is addressed.

Remember that GROW is merely a useful structure or system to assist the coaching process. Its power is that it is user-friendly and it works.

Uses of the Coaching Process and GROW

I used the process in almost every situation within my interaction with performers. The way I utilized the principles and process varied according to the situation and the person but they were always applicable. Some of the uses included:

- technical learning and improvement with individuals
- tactical awareness and performance at both small-group and team level
- development of teamworking both on and off the field
- set-piece creativity and implementation
- match strategies: evolution, communication and implementation
- development of the management team
- conflict resolution
- deselecting players
- strategic planning.

The process is highly flexible and adaptable but the real power is that it is the 'how-to' of empowerment. Coaches may have the best thought processes in the world but it is the performers who have to produce the results.

Involvement, understanding and ownership are recognized as essential cornerstones to high performance and I submit that these are best generated through the coaching process we have described.

CHAPTER SIX

So How Does a Team Grow?

Teams of Talent or Talented Teams

A group of talented performers cannot be assembled and then perform as a great team. It will be a team of great talent, probably very good but well below its potential.

Over time and with quality leadership and coaching this assembly of performers could evolve into a truly talented team. Now the team and the individuals are probably functioning much closer to their real potential. The added value is achieved through the work everyone chooses to give to the developing of all the interactions and interdependencies within the team. At first it may require a leap of faith but soon the rewards of improved team performance feed the need for a motive to give even more energy to the aspiration for excellence.

Sometimes a team of talent is enough to satisfy the aspirations of both the team leaders and the performers. Sport has plenty of teams who do not want to, or choose not to, give energy to real team development. They remain teams of talent. Each individual probably wants to perform well but primarily for himself. The team may be successful but there is something lacking. At the other extreme, there are teams who lack talented individuals and realize that their only route to achieve success is through teamwork. The energy they give to this does not guarantee success, but it often generates other things within the team, with the result that they achieve, as a team, more than they realistically could expect.

The simple reality is that a team may be assembled, but for it to become a team which performs close to its potential it has to be grown and nurtured.

Teams are living organisms which have the ability or capacity to change. They may grow strong or wither, be flexible or rigid, have complementary or competing sections, be energetic or lethargic, youthful or senile, be born or die. Teams have an organic growth about them and the challenge for team leaders and coaches is to work with them such that the teamwork, individuals' growth and team performance are brought to maturity together.

The more we see teams as having 'life' the more likely we are to work appropriately and assist them in their maturation, development, re-orientation, dying, rejuvenation and resurrection.

The Life Cycle of Teams

There are many models of team development that may be used to deepen an understanding of the life cycle of teams. The model I am offering is simple yet applicable to any group, team, sub-team or organization of any size. The simplicity of the three-stage model allows it to be easily understood and remembered and its universatility gives it great strength and validity.

The three stages are: *inclusion, assertion* and *co-operation*. The words illustrate the predominant needs of the people within each phase; *see* Figure 3.

This allows the model to be applied to an individual as well as a team and this fits perfectly with the coach's need to keep a focus upon each individual in order to build a team. The stages do not have distinct boundaries, each gradually merges into the next. The hypothesis is that as the team encourages and accommodates inclusion, assertion and co-operation the ability of the team to convert more of its potential into performance increases.

In Figure 4 a fourth column has been added to allow comparison of this model with some of the others that appear in books on team development. Most of the other models divide the co-operation stage into two. I stay with the three-stage cycle of development because of its simplicity and because both the underpinning needs and their resultant energy-focus cannot easily be subdivided further. I believe that 'needs' and 'energies' are the principal drivers in the development of teams. In their striving to promote real co-operation the best coaches identify them, influence them and work with them at both the individual and the team level.

Teams move through these phases in their natural evolution and, because teams are made up of individuals, one of the key challenges of the team coach is to enable individuals to make the journey into co-operation. But it is not possible to jump over a stage in this evolution, and so we

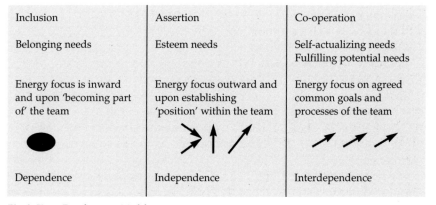

Inclusion	Assertion	Co-operation
Belonging needs	Esteem needs	Self-actualizing needs Fulfilling potential needs
Energy focus is inward and upon 'becoming part of' the team	Energy focus outward and upon establishing 'position' within the team	Energy focus on agreed common goals and processes of the team
Dependence	Independence	Interdependence

Fig. 3. Team Development Models

coaches are left with such problems as finding ways of accelerating or improving the smoothness of the process.

To add further complication the progress of individuals and teams may slow down, stop for a time or even regress. However, I hope to illustrate that a deeper understanding of what is going on within the team at each stage can greatly assist in the drive for high-quality team performance.

Inclusion	Assertion	Co-operation	
Forming	Storming	Norming	Performing
Confusion	Conflict	Co-operation	Commitment
Transactions	Self-expression	Mutuality	Alignment
Starting	Sorting	Stabilizing/striving	Succeeding

Fig. 4. Comparison of Team Development Models

Inclusion

Take your mind back to a time when you were a new member of a team, club or department. Or put yourself in the position of a new squad member coming to his first coaching or training session with your team or squad. What would be your feelings and thoughts then?

It is my experience that new members face discomfort and anxiety due to the questions they ask themselves, such as:

What is expected of me?
Am I the only 'new' member?
Will I be good enough?
Will I give a good account of myself?
Will I be accepted and liked by the others?
What are the squad rules?
Where do I fit in?
How can I fit in?

The answers to these questions and others are critical for the new member even though they may appear trivial to the experienced team member and coach. We can forget all too quickly these feelings and needs and fall into the trap of failing to deal with them properly.

Within this phase the need is to be included. The questions that arise in the players' minds focus their energies inwardly upon themselves, and while the energies are inward looking there can only be a limited orientation towards individual and team performance improvement.

It does not take long to provide positive answers to the needs of performers for inclusion, but unless it is done the advancement of the team may be inhibited.

How can we identify inclusion issues? First, an increased awareness in the coach of what may be the needs of a new team member, one returning to the team or of a newly-formed team will help. Secondly, there may be some indicators that provide insights. The following patterns of behaviour may be indicative of a need for action to generate greater inclusion:

- new or less experienced members practising, talking or socializing only with one another
- sub-groups within a team becoming too inward-looking
- new or less experienced members not able to provide input, not listened to or not shown value
- people in 'cover positions' are not clear about roles or procedures (for instance, No.2 line-out thrower in rugby)
- players unclear about one another's roles and responsibilities.

In addition, the need for inclusion, a decrease in the sense of belonging, may be generated by the actions of the coach; for example, the excluding of team members from situations in which they believe they should or could contribute. I excluded a squad member from a meeting of a sub-group of players that I saw as the more experienced performers. The reasons for this were fair and valid (to me, at least), but because he was feeling vulnerable about his future the move reinforced his anxiety. The outcome was that he needed further reassurance about his position (belonging needs) from me. Another process that may inhibit a sense of belonging is a delay in selection.

I am not so concerned about this on a match-to-match situation in teams where their interdependence is high, as is the case in, for example, soccer, rugby, hockey, basketball or netball. Here the issues are not so much about belonging to the squad – because they clearly do – but more about satisfying the need of the players to have the opportunity to show their ability (assertion needs). In the case of these teams it is the timing of the selection of the squad before a tournament that is worthy of consideration. If the selection is late then there is less time in which to move the selected squad through the evolutionary process, because it is not a case of simply carrying on from where the team's development had reached when the choices were made from the larger squad. In an amateur sport (hockey) in the 1980s I found that a twelve-week period with the selected squad of sixteen, meeting for perhaps twenty-five days in that time, seemed to work. Clearly, there is no scientific method of deciding this; only the experience that it is important to do.

However, if we take more individual sports that have team elements (athletics, squash, badminton, equestrian, fencing or tennis) it may be important to give more time and energy to the team's development as the level of interdependence during performance is relatively low.

The sense of belonging to a team may take more time and energy to generate. Without this sense of belonging, high performance through co-operation is unlikely to be achieved. Delaying selection will increase the pressure of time on the promotion of high-quality teamwork. This will inhibit the process and almost certainly result in performances that do not reflect the true potential of the team.

Within inclusion there is a considerable amount of dependence upon others to do the including. It is difficult as a new member of a team to include oneself. We can introduce ourselves and make efforts to be open and friendly, yet to be included we are dependent upon others. In fact, the act of trying too hard to include ourselves may generate feelings in people that inhibit the very process of inclusion.

- What do you set up to help new members to feel included?
- What do the more experienced players do?
- What could be done to improve the way you address inclusion issues?
- What inclusion issues exist in your squad or team at present?
- What are the effects of deselection on the performer? Is he still part of the squad or team? How may he still feel included?

Inclusion needs are not confined to team members alone, team leaders may also experience their negative effects. Look back at the questions that illustrated some of the anxieties facing new team members and imagine yourself as a newly-appointed leader. How many of these might apply to a new leader? Probably more than we would at first think. Certainly the following thoughts might arise:

- What is expected of me?
- How will I achieve the standards of my predecessor?
- Will I give a good account of myself?
- Will I be accepted/respected/trusted?

Such questions and anxieties turn the energies of the person inward, and in leadership positions the need is to enable energies to be focused outward on the team and its objectives. People taking on new leadership roles may also require help to overcome these problems.

Now, what if you are appointing a new manager, assistant coach, doctor, physiotherapist or captain – what would you do to minimize the potentially negative effect of these anxieties?

Assertion

Once many of the inclusion needs have been satisfied the next level of need comes to the forefront and demands attention. This is the need in the performer to contribute and be recognized for this contribution; it is the drive to demonstrate that he has something to offer and be valued for that, to find his position within the team and for that to be acknowledged by the team. The energies and behaviour are orientated to the satisfaction of these assertion needs: to establish a position within the team and to receive the esteem of others for his contribution.

Within this phase much of the energy is outward, but when it is left to its own devices it is often more orientated to establishing position *vis-à-vis* other team members than in moving forward the level of co-operation. People are asserting their independence and exerting their power to achieve it. There is nothing inherently wrong in this since it is a natural process within the human and the animal world. We may not like some of the negative behaviours that may occur as a result of such assertion, but that should not lead us to damn assertion itself. If we do that we inhibit the growth of the individual or the team as an entity. To condemn compet-itive team sports because of some negative player attitudes or behaviour or the results of poorly-managed competition makes little sense. Competition exists in the life of any organism.

People may compete with, challenge or indulge in conflict with others in their search for position and then defend it aggressively. Such behav-iour may be aimed at anyone in the team or even the leadership and be either overt or covert. The fact is that some of the things we do in order to satisfy inclusion needs actually begin the assertion drive and promote independence. Providing a role for someone, telling him what he has to offer the team and what is expected of him all go to make him feel that he belongs and yet also stimulate the drive to establish a position in the team. And it is correct that we should do this because the only route to high co-operation is through the promoting of independence. Only when people have asserted their independence can they choose to be truly co-operative. It is imperative in team coaching to work to orientate and channel the evidence from behaviour in the assertion phase towards increased co-operation, to see assertive actions as stepping stones to co-operative actions rather than as inhibitors to teamwork. Some of these behaviours will be more challenging than others to change while others will be so negative as to require drastic action.

The player who beats two others but holds on to the ball to beat a third and fails is illustrating assertive behaviour. However, the real issue is related to his behaviour as he approached the third player, for releasing the ball prior to that would have been very effective for the team. There are performers who are more focused on their own per-formance than on that of the team. Losing is not an issue provided that they played well, because then the loss is no fault of theirs.

How we deal with these and other assertion issues will vary according to the individual and the situation, but if we seek to promote or even accelerate co-operation and high team performance we cannot simply leave it to natural evolution. To be perverse, there may be times when the best thing to do is to leave things as they are. Many rather 'individualistic' performers are difficult to handle because they are highly talented yet need to assert their individualism all too often. Sometimes during performances other players manage these assertive behaviours better than the coaches and managers. They may protect or support the over-assertive, talented performer when he continually gets involved with referees or opponents. Players are often willing to do this while the difficult player continues to produce high-quality results. However, as the performance of that player drops so does the support. In this case the best use of the coach's energies is to help the other players cope and watch for indicators in the performance of the difficult player, since as soon as it declines all the problems the other players have with him will flood to the surface.

Within the assertion phase there is every possibility that some of the potentially most negative energy will be generated as a result of competition, confrontation and sub-groups. These are key processes and will be dealt with later in the chapter. In the meantime let us move the team onward and upward.

Co-operation

As performers find their position through their independent contribution and the recognition of this by others, so their willingness to acknowledge the needs of others and of the team increases. Players begin to choose to perform their roles in ways that satisfy the team's needs rather than their own. They work with each other in ways that illustrate much greater openness, trust and support.

The driving need that prompts this change of approach is related to the desire to fulfil potential: to convert potential into actual performance. Players not only recognize that in using their talents more co-operatively they can achieve an improved performance, but also decide to behave accordingly. Their energies are more focused upon objectives and processes agreed upon by the team to be important in achieving high performance. Essentially, people choose to co-operate and the overriding emphasis in their interactions and relationships is one of interdependence. In this phase the players illustrate that the team is more important than the individual through their willingness to co-operate.

One of the most effective ways to identify behaviours associated with the co-operation phase is to reflect on the qualities that a high-performing team illustrates. Before you review the list below, recall a high-

performance team with which you have been closely associated and identify a few of the qualities or characteristics which that team exhibited.

The very best teams are characterized by qualities such as:

- high-quality support
- good leadership
- mutual trust and respect
- encouragement
- risks allowed
- no blame
- positive competition
- focus on common goals
- clear roles and responsibilities
- clear lines of communication
- good communication processes
- high-quality skills
- good balance of talents
- ability to change the pace of play
- variety of personalities
- personal and team responsibilities accepted
- high expectations set by performers of themselves
- the will to win
- commitment
- honesty
- openness
- unity of purpose
- clear personal goals that support team goals.

Study your own conclusions along with the above and then spend at
least 15 minutes doing the following activity (use Table 4 as a template):

1. Reflect on your present team or squad and list the qualities you
   believe are especially important to have if your team is going to
   be the best it could be; not all of the generic qualities listed above
   will be a priority for your team and your sport.
2. Now rate the team on each of these qualities (using a 1 to 10 scale)
   as you see it now.
3. Identify the qualities which you believe are the most important
   ones to address to help the team improve its performance.
4. For these chosen qualities, decide what the realistic yet
   challenging future rating, on the same scale, you would like to
   achieve with this team and on the timescale in which you would
   like to see it achieved.
5. For each of these qualities identify a specific behaviour or action

that would be happening in the team if it were exhibiting the quality to the higher score (the future target).

6. To translate this to the personal level use Table 5 to identify what you are going to do differently to contribute to an improvement.

This activity may be completed both by the team coaches or managers and the team itself in a variety of ways. The power of this kind of process is that it:

- demands a focus upon prioritizing the qualities and characteristics of a high-performing team in a particular sport
- generates the qualities and characteristics against which progress may be measured
- has a positive and future focus
- translates qualities into actual behaviours and actions
- actively promotes the process of generating co-operation.

Clearly many of the qualities of a highly co-operative team are aspirations towards which we attempt to make as rapid progress as possible. Some of them are reasonably tangible and finite, for instance, goals and responsibilities, whereas others are much more nebulous, such as

Team quality	Present rating	Future target	Time scale	Behaviours that would reflect the 'future target'

Table 4. Evaluating the Qualities of Your Team

commitment and good leadership. Of course, these variations make such qualities challenging to track as we progress as a team and, because of this perceived difficulty in observing and measuring these qualities, they are not overtly developed. The result is that too many teams miss the opportunity to fulfil their potential properly because they do not actively seek to take the prime co-operative qualities to the highest possible level. In some teams there may be good reasons for this action and in these cases it is a conscious decision. However, in the majority of teams the reason is the failure to tackle the issues rather than in choosing not to open them up.

It is a dangerous tactic as a team developer to work only at the inclusion and assertion issues in the hope that these will in themselves somehow bring the team to the promised land of co-operation. I see the process from another perspective. My intention is to work with them such that they can become a really good team. Therefore the first step is to try to identify what that team would look like in the co-operation phase. By doing this we not only create a positive picture towards which we all work, but also we facilitate the establishing of observable and measurable criteria against which we can evaluate the process of team development. Within this context the challenges of inclusion and assertion may be viewed in a different light. They are merely blockages or nuisances along a reasonably clear pathway,

Team quality	Behaviours that would reflect the 'future target'	My present rating	Future target	Measures of success: what I am going to do differently

Table 5. Personal Development in the Agreed Qualities

as opposed to blockages to our being able to find the pathway and see the goal.

Study your list of the qualities of a high-performing team in your sport. In how many of these could you put some aspect in place early in the developmental cycle of the team? Common goals, clear roles and defined responsibilities could be agreed upon quite quickly, thus providing three key qualities on which both the team and the individual members may focus. Having these in place does not guarantee improved teamwork but it almost certainly fosters the process. But what else might you do? What if you were to begin to promote such qualities as 'no blame' or 'high-level support'? What could you, as the coach, actively do to promote the kinds of behaviour that would encourage these qualities to a high level?

Take a quality from your list which you would like to see at a heightened level in your team. What could you do with your performers to promote an improvement in this quality?

Through this process I have found that there are many things I could do to actively encourage team members to move towards a more co-operative way of working. We can be models of the quality we want to promote. If I want to generate trust then my showing trustworthiness is an important part of the process. Openness cannot be promoted if I am secretive.

This process is not a complete answer in itself because the team members themselves must decide to work with one another in line with these qualities. However, being congruent with them in our work with the performers increases the likelihood of the qualities taking root and growing. In addition, if the performances are reviewed in the light of the key qualities we wish to develop then this reinforces the growth of both the specific qualities and the co-operative process. (We not only gain an improvement in trust but also become more co-operative in the process.)

The power and effectiveness of the co-operation phase is such that it acknowledges, allows and supports the existence of both inclusion and assertion. While the energies may be focused on the main team goals and processes, personal achievements aligned to these (goals) are allowed to which individuals are able to give their energies simultaneously. In this way interdependence acknowledges the importance of independence and encourages it. The highly co-operative team has both the focus and the processes to work positively with assertion and inclusion issues.

It would be pleasant to think that once the challenges of inclusion and assertion issues have been addressed then the path ahead is one only of degrees of co-operation. The reality is that there are on-going challenges to team development which may not only inhibit advancement but also cause the team to regress.

CHAPTER SEVEN

Competition, Confrontation and Sub-Groups

Challenges to Positive Growth

If causing teams to evolve towards high-quality co-operation were easy then there would be no place for books such as this. The experiences gained from years of involvement with teams would be of little value. The growth and progress with our teams would be predictable provided that we followed the plan or model. Clearly, and thankfully, this is not the case.

Teams are the manifestation of individuals choosing to try and work together to achieve things for which they require one another's energies. They are also visible expression of our dreams, hopes and ambitions. They are living organisms that are influenced by internal and external forces. When I view teams in this way, I find my imagination unlocked and my energies ignited by my desire to be involved. I am also in awe of the potential complexity of the challenge and wonder how on earth they ever work as well as they do.

Imagine trying to put together an entity when, although you have the plan for it and the tools, all the components have varying aspirations, needs, ambitions, qualities and characteristics: that summarizes teams.

The factors that can inhibit team growth may be at both the macro and the micro level. At the former it could be that issues such as competition, confrontation and sub-groupings are manifesting themselves in the team with negative consequences. On the other hand, there are factors which may appear at an individual level that may adversely affect team development. These may include loss of form, new team members, deselection or loss of confidence. To complicate matters, the source of these inhibiting factors may be within the individual, within the team, within the management or outside the immediate team environment.

In the following sections I examine some of these factors. I cannot cover all of them and you may find many others more specific to your situation, your team and your sport.

Competition, confrontation and sub-groupings are interactions that commonly occur in teams and are inescapable aspects of being human. On the one hand they are perfectly normal happenings within human groups, while on the other they have the potential to inhibit team co-operation. The challenge for the coach is to work with the energies that naturally occur within the team and the harnessing of these is the most positive way for the advancement of the team.

Competition

Competition is seen primarily as an assertive behaviour. It is driven by a desire to match our standards against those set by others in the same field of performance. When competition is viewed within this setting it becomes much more valuable to the team coach, because to challenge ourselves against the standards of others in our field – particularly of those who establish standards – is imperative for performance improvement. Competition may not be attractive; it is essential!

It is not the desire to compete that is the inhibitor of team co-operation but more the motive for the competition and the way the consequences of it are handled. The negative side of competition within a team, or between teams in the same organization, is that it can generate:

- negative energy between people
- the withholding of information for individual gain
- personal agendas focused upon succeeding at any cost
- the 'winners' and 'losers' syndrome
- energy focused upon personal position rather than performance
- loss of respect and trust between people.

These are all motives and consequences that any coach would seek to minimize in the process of building a team. However, on the positive side competition can engender:

- high standards of performance
- personal agendas focused upon aspiring to be the best they can be
- recognition based upon performance criteria rather than personal position
- acknowledgement and respect of the differences between colleagues.

As a coach, I would want to have plenty of these positives. It is not competition that is the difficulty, rather the way that we handle it. The best coaches recognize the position and power of the competitive drive in humans and seek to orientate it away from the negatives and towards the positives. The process of doing this, or of attempting to, will contribute towards the promoting of greater co-operation, because the actions of the coach will be mirroring many of the qualities known to be essential in a high-performing team. Confirm this for yourself; if you were working with your team to promote the positive outcomes of internal competition:

- what would you be doing specifically (behaviours)?
- which qualities from your list of the qualities of a high-performing team would those behaviours be supporting positively?

The best teams – those working within the co-operation phase – not only deal with internal competition more effectively but also welcome it. To a high-performing team, internal competition is about sustaining and advancing the standards that enable it to challenge itself to perform against other teams in its field.

The 'squad system' in sports attempts to achieve this position of high co-operation in a group of players that is obviously larger than the team itself. Every member has the desire to play himself and yet is willing to contribute to team success irrespective of his selection. This may appear idealistic but the very best teams have tackled these apparent paradoxes. If we as team coaches and managers do not believe it is possible to find the best solutions to these dilemmas, I wonder whether we shall get even halfway there.

In the inclusion and assertion phases internal competition has a propensity to shift towards negative outcomes. This is because much of the energy of the individual is focused upon himself. In inclusion it is about belonging and being accepted, while in assertion the need for personal contribution and recognition comes to the forefront. In the former, competition may appear when someone new tries to include himself or attempts to push his talents forward uninvited. Often this results only in exclusion.

In the assertion phase competition comes to the fore and the examples are clear for all to see. In both phases, however, the team may not be able to deal positively with the potential effects of competition without significant outside assistance from the coach or manager. I would go so far as to say that, even though there will be present some more mature members possibly capable of assisting the process, it is the responsibility of the management to lead and drive that process.

While the most critical challenges to the coach with regard to the effect of competition within the team or squad lie in the inclusion and the assertion phase, we must not close our minds to dealing even more effectively with it in a high-performing team.

Before the British Lions tour of South Africa in 1997 an old friend, Geoff Jackson, led the team development work that Impact (the management development company) did with the squad. At one point they facilitated a discussion between the players who were 'competing' for the same positions on the field: while there are special circumstances surrounding a touring squad that plays mid-week and weekend matches, this kind of discussion provides the opportunity to face reality and find positive ways forwards. In isolation it is merely an example of confronting the competition/co-operation issue. When combined with all the other pieces of the jigsaw put in place by the 1997 Lions it contributed to a powerful performance in every aspect. At this level, co-operation and interdependence are attitudes of mind that underpin and drive everything put in place to achieve the common goals.

Confrontation

Confrontation and competition may be seen as slightly differing aspects of the need in the human to challenge. So is challenge through confrontation or conflict a thing we should avoid? On the one hand confrontations serve to challenge the reasons for doing things in a certain way and demand that energy is taken away from moving forward. This may be frustrating and time-consuming. On the other hand few performance enhancements that are worthwhile come about through a process lacking in confrontation. Yet again the coach is in the world of understanding the potential pitfalls and gains from the natural flows of energy within a team. Confronting ourselves and one another may be seen as both imperative and inhibiting.

What might be negative outcomes of confrontation between the members of your team or between yourself as coach and the team? What might be the positive outcomes of confronting the issues?

Now that you can see what could happen consider what you would do as the leader of this process to maximize the opportunities for positive outcomes. See Figure 5.

In order to promote positive outcomes from the process of confronting issues, I shall do the following:

*

*

*

*

*

*

Fig. 5. Confronting Issues with my Team/Squad

Sub-groupings

The formation of these is perhaps the most natural process in all but the smallest teams. All large 'teams' have historically been subdivided into smaller units or sub-teams. The reasons for this are a mixture of the organizational, ease of effectiveness of communication, recognition and energy focus. All these important issues can be dealt with very well with smaller numbers and to the benefit of the whole team.

Some of these sub-groupings are formalized through the structure of the teams (forwards and specialist units, for instance) while others are more informal (such as the senior players or common interest groups). They exist and always will.

The positive contributions of sub-groups include:

- the capacity to focus on highly specialized areas for whole team
- the effective use of resources and interests
- they offer a clear sense of belonging to any 'new' members
- they allow development along several fronts simultaneously
- they reduce the chances of the exclusion of individuals.

On the debit side, sub-groups offer the potential for:

- cliques with their own agenda to establish themselves
- the team may lose the key focus
- parts of the team may become isolated or excluded.

Within the inclusion phase new members, if their need to be accepted is not addressed, may form a sub-group based upon this common experience. The negative consequences of competition and confrontation also have the potential to cause sub-groupings of disappointed and de-motivated performers.

Teams within teams, which is another way of looking at many of the sub-groups, are perfectly normal and ought to be encouraged. The one single and most important principle is that their work must contribute positively to both the teamworking and the team performance.

Spend some moments reflecting on your team:

- how may sub-groups exist:
  in the playing team?
  informally, when the team is not performing?
- what positive contributions do these sub-teams make to team performance?
- what is happening, if anything, in the team that might cause negative consequences in any sub-group?

CHAPTER EIGHT

Some Other Potential Challenges to Team Growth

New Members

Anyone who has experienced being a new member of an existing team will understand the feelings of being on the outside, wondering whether acceptance will occur and if so when and how. Although these issues exist for the new team members, other things may be happening which warrant attention too. New members are focused upon themselves and their position rather than the team's outputs. This probably has the impact of lowering the performance or effectiveness of the team. The more experienced and mature members may choose to continue to focus upon sustaining team performance and ignore the giving of energy to the new members. The danger here is that if the new members are not effectively included and provided with the opportunity to generate a real contribution, other members of the team will face frustrations.

Team performance will be sustained only through their increased application and energy, while the new members are unable to contribute significantly. The result can be that the existing members, or some of them, see their new colleagues as not contributing sufficiently to team performance. The effect will be misdirected energy within the team and a focus upon the lack of effective input from new people or insufficient support by the more experienced members. The outcome will almost certainly be inhibiting to team growth until the real issues are resolved. New members need to be included properly and allowed to establish themselves as quickly as possible. The more experienced members need to be aware of the challenges to the team and their responsibilities in making the transition as soon as possible. The team leader has a major part to play in facilitating this process even though many of the necessary actions will be in the control of the team members themselves.

In integrating new team members:

What do you do to integrate new members effectively into your team or squad?
What works well?
What will you consider doing differently in the future?

Loss of Form

Consider what happens to an individual when his or her performance is below normal. At first the difficulties can be assessed and appropriate actions determined that, it is to be hoped, remedy the situation. But what if it continues?

The loss of effectiveness causes the energies of the person to turn inward. This introspection will in itself not be negative, while the context remains one of finding ways to sustain and improve the most useful contribution to the team's goals. However, it does not take a great deal of negative self-talk to alter this situation.

Concern about where this loss of form places the performer with regard to other team members and, in particular, people who might perform in his or her position may rapidly shift the context into one of self-assertion. This change may result in behaviour more orientated to the re-establishing of a personal position rather than to team development. Even greater concerns may arise within the person linked to his or her ability to perform to the required level or to being excluded. Now look where they have slipped: towards inclusion.

It is not that a loss of form always causes these changes or that they are easy to recognize. The important learning for team coaches and managers is to understand the potential impact of a loss of form on both the individual's and the team's performance. If we understand more clearly the likely causes of the behaviour of players who experience a loss of form we have the opportunity to tackle them. The ability to treat the causes as well as the symptoms can accelerate the growth of both the individual and the team.

Taking this to a micro level within a game, it could be argued that the players who attempt to rectify previous errors in judgement with a more audacious piece of play are experiencing the same process. The high-risk strategy is designed and attempted more to re-establish themselves in one step than to advance the team. The 'symptom' is an ill-judged action, but the 'cause' is the response to previous disappointments. The underlying cause is the one coaches often fail to understand and to find ways to improve.

Run of Poor Team Results

'Winning is a habit.' This is a remark often paraded by coaches when they are trying to explain a run of good or of disappointing results. But what does it really mean?

My experience tells me that it is about the attitudinal changes that can come about from success. Not only do we draw out the learning but we also continually apply it to subsequent competition, and in doing so we increase our opportunities to succeed, which in their turn positively influence our belief that we shall succeed (*see* Figure 6). Of course, we also have to have the fundamental abilities appropriate to high team performance – skills, experiences, fitness, strategy and tactics – and the willingness to work co-operatively if we aspire to sustained success.

Your answers to these issues will provide insights into what happens at present, what you would like to see occurring in the future, and how you might move forward.

Delaying Selection

This is often seen as a good tactic for keeping the players on their toes and not allowing them to become complacent about their selection. My experience is that there are subtle yet important differences in the application of this tactic which can have powerful effects on both the individuals and the team. Delaying the selection of a match team from a squad at a tournament is different from delaying the announcement of the squad for the tournament.

Let me take the former situation first. Whatever the reasons for the delay in the selection of the match team, one hopes that the quality of the team-working developed during squad preparation enables the performers to

What has been the impact of the run of poor results on:

    the way the team works together:

        in training?

        before a match?

        during the match?

        post-match?

    individuals within the team (positive and negative)?

    the coaching team?

    the head coach?

What has been your response to the poor results?

What specific behaviours do you want to see in the team or squad that would help the situation?

What could you personally do to help to promote these behaviours/characteristics?

In what ways could you involve the team or squad in finding some ways forward?

Fig.6. Exploring the Effects of Poor Results on Team Cohesion

overcome any feelings of uncertainty. In addition, if performers know that later rather than earlier selection is the norm then the potential difficulties are reduced. The reason the squad can accommodate this process is because its growth has established high levels of co-operation.

However, delaying the selection of the squad may create significant difficulties because the players may have been more interested in asserting their position – to gain selection – than in promoting high-quality co-operation. The performers do not feel secure and the delay exacerbates this situation. Only when the selection has been completed can the all-important work of promoting successful teamwork begin in earnest.

This process is a balancing act in which the coaches of national teams are continually engaged. The greater the need for detailed, intensive, high-quality interaction to achieve the necessary teamwork, the more important it is to select the squad earlier rather than later.

At club level the timing of selection may have to take account of other things, such as having the appropriate people practising together on the training evening, how long before the match the playing squad assembles or how much time the coach wants the players to have to prepare themselves for competition.

It is not that one way is right and another wrong. The most important thing is for the coach to recognize the effects on the performers of the timing of the selection process.

But delayed selection has the potential to:

- hold players in assertive behaviour focused on establishing or confirming a favourable position in the squad
- emphasize competitiveness in a winner/loser vein
- inhibit co-operative activity
- increase anxiety and uncertainty
- promote independent rather than interdependent attitudes.

I have experienced many variations on this theme as both player and coach. I notice that I tried to weigh up what was best for any given situation, bearing in mind that my overriding responsibility was to get the best possible team prepared in the best possible way to tackle the challenges ahead. As I became more aware of the ramifications of the timing of selection so I made better decisions for the team or squad.

Climate of Fear

Coaches who cause performers to be fearful may feel powerful but in reality it is an abuse of power. To help players to perform to a high standard demands that coaches promote the personal power of the performer. Only when the players truly own what they do will they be able to respond to the dynamic situation of the game; in other words, be free to respond in the best possible way. When people choose their responses to situations they almost certainly accept accountability for their decisions. All too often the holding of people accountable is used to direct blame. In these situations the purpose of accountability is to establish blame. This puts 'blame' as the central issue and therefore the most powerful factor in the coach–performer interactions. Performers in their desire to avoid the experience of being blamed shy away from accepting responsibility. Their reasoning is sound: why take responsibility for something which, if it does not go well (even though you may not have control over all the relevant factors), will be blamed on you personally? Sound reasoning yet poor outcome.

Choosing to accept responsibility generates real accountability, being willing to be held accountable. A culture of fear and blame does not provide people with any feeling of real choice, with the result that their level of ownership is low. They can still be held accountable but their acceptance of it is much lower. This is evidenced by the numerous valid reasons, excuses and mitigating circumstances they provide.

In reality, the apportionment of blame is a response to the outcome of performance whereas accountability is much more concerned with the acceptance of responsibility of the process involved in the performance. 'It was your fault that you missed the goal and lost the match', rather than, 'I saw the opening for a shot a little too late and it caused me to rush my one chance of a goal.'

Blame is usually imposed from 'outside' whereas accountability is accepted from the 'inside'. Blame is the punishment for not achieving and generates self-justification, convergent analysis and negative judgements. Real accountability is the acknowledgement of a contribution and this generates description and learning.

Punishment may promote fear of failure, which is a somewhat negative goal and therefore not a useful focus for performers. This is quite different from the understandable and perfectly normal apprehension performers feel when they face the challenge to succeed. Both can be generated but the second is a much better use of the 'fear' factor.

This is the difference between fear being your 'friend' and your 'foe'. Coaches have choice in how they make use of the 'power' vested in them and the natural 'fears' regarding performance that reside in the performers. My experience has shown that the long-term growth and achievement of performers is enhanced significantly if their personal (team) power is developed. The process does not lessen the power of the coach nor diminish his accountability; it merely, yet crucially, devolves responsibility for the process of performance to where it truly belongs – with the performer.

Promoting Co-operation within the Life-cycle of a Squad

There is a natural life-cycle of a squad of performers. Within Olympic sports this is often a four-year cycle encompassing one Olympic Games. For other sports it may cover the world championship cycle which may be every two or four years. Even within a four-year cycle there are micro cycles of perhaps one year or one season.

Whatever the length of the cycle you experience in your sport, there will be clear phases that differ significantly from one another in the challenges they pose in generating team co-operation. The coach is engaged in the challenge of leading the development of the squad in all aspects of team growth: technical and tactical, individual and group, physiological and psychological, and attitudinal and behavioural.

My challenge to you in this section is to apply your learning and experience of teams and their development towards being highly co-operative.

The Phases of the Life-cycle

Only you can identify the phases for your squad in your sport. To illustrate what I mean by phases, I noticed within the final year before the 1988 Olympic Games that the phases were as shown in Figure 7.

Within each of these phases there were key issues materializing concerning 'inclusion', 'assertion' and 'co-operation' that were reasonably predictable given an understanding of the people involved and the way humans behave in teams. Strategies and tactics had to be formulated to find positive solutions that both addressed the issues and enabled the team to develop. We did not find all the best answers, but by being more purposeful in our thinking we probably identified many of them.

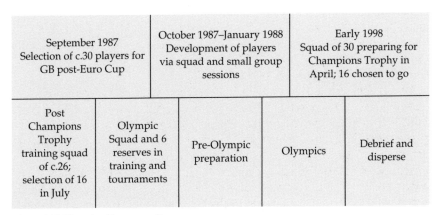

September 1987 Selection of c.30 players for GB post-Euro Cup	October 1987–January 1988 Development of players via squad and small group sessions	Early 1998 Squad of 30 preparing for Champions Trophy in April; 16 chosen to go		
Post Champions Trophy training squad of c.26; selection of 16 in July	Olympic Squad and 6 reserves in training and tournaments	Pre-Olympic preparation	Olympics	Debrief and disperse

Fig.7. 1988 Olympics: Pre-games Phases

From Table 6 see whether you can identify within each phase:
- the words that describe the phase (or sub-phase)
- the key issues that are likely to arise
- some strategies that would help you reduce the negative side of the issues and to generate greater co-operation.

I have put a few of the details from my first phase as an illustration.

Phase	Key team development issues likely to arise	Strategies for coping with issues and promoting greater co-operation
1. Selection and bringing together an initial training squad of 30 players	Inclusion issues particularly for younger members Individual focusing on themselves, uncertainty or personal agendas No idea of exactly where they stand in the squad	Outline purpose of squad Involve squad in development of strategies, tactics, team behaviour Mix old and young players both on and off practice ground Clarify roles/expectations as much as possible Illustrate openness of opportunity for all Actively involve younger/new players
2. Development of all players at squad and small group sessions		
3. Squad training for Tournament with selection of 16 from 30		

Table 6. Key issues with Phases of Team Development

CHAPTER NINE

Motivation and Team Performance

It is within the area of motivation that some of the obvious paradoxes between the individual and the team appear most clearly: 'If you want to develop a strong team keep close attention to the individual.' This statement, while apparently paradoxical, is powerfully true when one actively works with teams. Every team development has to be agreed and implemented at the individual level if it is to be truly effective and add value to team performance. This does not mean that every team member must be party to every discussion. That would be admirable and ideal yet often not practicable. However, it does mean that, unless all team members choose to accept the potential improvement as valid and valuable, it is unlikely to be implemented with the necessary degree of focus, energy and enthusiasm to ensure its success.

Motivation is defined simply as 'supplying a motive to a person': a motive is 'an inducement to a person or act'. Self-motivation is 'acting on one's own initiative'. Team coaches are immersed in this challenging area of motivation in everything they do because there is no simple definition or process of team motivation.

The coach's principal goal is team performance and therefore if we link our work to the team development model the motive that drives the coach must be 'to generate both for and with his performers that which encourages and promotes co-operation'. This sounds to be of general applicability and yet it is valid for any piece of work I do with a team. From broad strategies to specific small-group interactions; from team rules to individual disciplines; from team goals to personal review sessions, in any area my higher goal is to promote and generate team co-operation.

At another level it may be necessary for the coach to work with an individual or small group to enable him or them to improve. This may require their finding the motive for change, but if this motive is not in alignment with the generating of greater co-operation then it is likely to inhibit rather than promote team performance. This is the core work of a team coach in the sphere of motivation. To generate in the performers a willingness to act in the interests of the team rather than for self-interest. It is the process of promoting the shifts in energy shown in Figure 8.

Of course, the very best teams manifest enormous energy focused upon

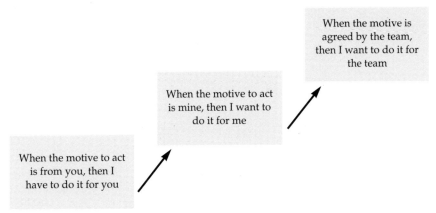

Fig.8. Motives and Energy Shifts

performing for the team, and yet within this individuals are encouraged to flourish and be themselves. The most co-operative teams allow individualism because it has been accommodated through co-operative processes. Throughout my work in hockey I aspired to help the players to create 'a talented team' rather than just 'a team of talent'. It is my experience that the former emerges only when the team truly enters the co-operative phase described earlier.

Within your team try to identify what would be different if it were operating as a talented team. This may provide some important insights.

What Is It that Motivates People?

If generating motives or inducements to act is such a strong thread that runs through all the work of a coach then perhaps we need to be clear on what does motivate our performers.

For the purpose of this explanation I shall stay at the general level, whereas when we apply the concepts to our performers we shall automatically drop into specific detail.

Inner and Outer

When people are asked, 'What motivates you to perform to your best?' they often give an interesting range of responses. Some I have experienced over the last ten years of running workshops on coaching, teams and performance are shown in Figure 9.

All these are recognizable as real motives that could induce a person to act. Now look a little closer: there is a simple yet powerful difference between the upper and the lower grouping. The upper group comprises motives that are generated from within the person whereas the lower motives come from outside. Which group do you think is the more powerful and longer-lasting in promoting performance improvement?

The intrinsic motivators win this contest easily. Not because the extrinsic motives are weak, but because the intrinsic ones cause the person to want to do it for himself. This generates much more positive energy than having to do if for someone else. This recognition neither diminishes nor devalues the extrinsic motivators, it merely puts them in their position relative to the intrinsic drivers. While it is generally acknowledged that the intrinsic motives are the ones we most want to foster, the extrinsic cannot be ignored. The truth is that the only motives the coach has within his control are the extrinsic ones. But before we tackle that dilemma let us explore the outer and the inner motives more deeply.

The Outer Drivers

The extrinsic motivators such as fear, money or praise can be powerful currencies but they may also be short-lived in duration or insufficient on their own.

One can always get a performance out of someone if you put fear into him. A gun to the head will always produce performance. However, the next time that you try with the gun you may find that he is no longer around or is bobbing and weaving to avoid you. The consequence is always misplaced energy and focus and sub-maximal performance. Even the reward of money can only go so far to motivate a person because in time we find that he values something more than he does the extra money. Lastly, even praise when it comes from outside the performer may result in diminishing returns if used inappropriately. The teacher who continually praises children no matter what they do soon finds that the currency of praise is devalued, and when it means nothing to the recipients it no longer acts as a motive for them to improve their performance.

For many years, the main extrinsic motivators were variations on the

challenge myself	achieve success
pride	improve performance
sense of self-worth	develop new skills
for the team	self-satisfaction
sense of belonging	do the job well
new learning	
promotion	recognition of others
fear	peer pressure
selection	money
	status symbols

Fig. 9. Performer Motivation

well-known carrot-and-stick process. The inducements were dangled in front of us to motivate us to higher performance while, just in case these were insufficient, the stick hovered threateningly behind. There were times even when the carrot itself turned into a stick to beat us with when we were unable to reach it, such as training schedules designed to help and then league tables of monitoring. Of course, this motivating metaphor originated in our attempt to promote a better performance with donkeys. But perhaps donkeys have never been an inspiring sight with regard to high performance and it is interesting that we have clung to the form of motivation thought appropriate for them in our desire to inspire humans.

I would assume that if you treat people like donkeys they then tend to perform like them, doing only as little as possible and even that in a grudging manner. This is not to say that this extrinsic motivator is not powerful and not useful. Money, promotion, status recognition, company cars and incentive schemes are all powerful, extrinsic motivators. However, while they remain that, although they may be powerful for some, for the majority they are only a part of their motivation to perform well since without an increase in the personal ownership of a motive by the performer himself, they remain far less influential than they might be.

To return to the list of motives given by individuals, a further pattern may be found within the intrinsic group. This is shown in Figure 10.

The Inner Drivers

It could be said that there are three core intrinsic drivers within the human being which seem to be with us from the moment we are born to the time

Performance
- achieve success
- improve performance
- do the job well

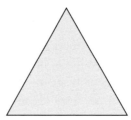

Fig.10. Performance, Learning and Enjoyment

Enjoyment
- pride and self-satisfaction
- self-worth
- team work
- sense of belonging

Learning
- challenge myself
- develop new skills
- new learning

we die. These could be labeled *performance, learning* and *enjoyment*. When we look at the motives for the actions that we take on our own initiative, we find that almost all can be placed within one of these categories. No one category is more important than another, but each person may have a differing balance in terms of the importance of each of the drivers in formulating the motives behind his or her actions. In other words, what drives you from within will be different to what drives me. *Performance* is about the goal or achievement orientation of the human being. It is probably the performance urge which causes children to get up and walk or learn to ride a bicycle. They are not instructed in how to do it but for some reason are driven, perhaps by a desire for movement or to get somewhere faster. It is the motive behind people who want to do the job better or to do it more effectively. Perhaps even it is one of the motives that drive people to climb mountains. When asked the reason, they often reply with words to the effect of 'because it was there'. It seems a strange answer but perhaps it is not.

These drives are in all people at some time or another. I doubt whether anyone enters a new job without the determination to do it well. We may ask a few weeks later what became of that first, positive drive, but that may be more an indictment of the way he has been worked with than of the motives that first drove him from within. People who have a strong performance drive within them may be more action-orientated than others. They are interested in goals and targets aimed at improving things as they do them.

The second driver within the human being is *learning*. This is the curiosity of the child, the desire to explore and challenge himself. In adult life this manifests itself in a person's need for new challenges or a desire to constantly accommodate new learning. Interestingly, this drive is evident within people when we look at their lives in total, as all too often we perhaps see it missing in the workplace. People take on enormous challenges in their hobbies and passions outside work, perhaps accepting responsibility far in excess of that which they achieve at work. People often retire and then go on and do quite astounding things regarding their ability to learn, even though they are late in life. This should be a salutary lesson for those of us involved in promoting high performance in both ourselves and others. The capacity to learn is there within us and our challenge is to promote our willingness to provide opportunity and encourage their willingness to accept it. 'Old dogs' can learn new tricks; the key is the willingness of the 'old dog' to learn.

The third intrinsic driver within people is to do with *enjoyment*. This is not just having fun, although in the child this hedonistic drive is an important one in their achievement of improved performance. Enjoyment is the feeling that people gain from the process of performing. These feelings of well-being can be given by people to themselves. This is the esteem they confer on themselves and may manifest itself in a feeling of pride, satisfaction or a feeling of belonging to or of commitment to a team. These feelings can, of course, be positively influenced by the way in which esteem is shown to them by others.

While the enjoyment drive is often seen as the soft area of motivation, I find in all the workshops I run that the list of words which fall under 'enjoyment' is longer than is the case in the other two areas. Interestingly, in the reality of life the motives of pride, satisfaction, sense of belonging, loyalty and recognition of one's own ability in a job are powerful in our desire to perform well.

Of course, our motivation is influenced by all three areas. Although there will be subtle variations between people, the more we understand about the prime intrinsic motives which drive people the more we can help them to tap into these powerful drivers. It would be inappropriate to focus only upon one of these areas, for example, to implore people constantly to perform and perform. While this focus and desire to tap into the performance drive of people would work for some it would be far less effective for others. All too often in the past we have aspired to gain access to this motivator alone. We are now beginning to recognize that the only way we can truly promote continuous performance improvement is to utilize all three intrinsic drivers. Only when we do this are we likely to achieve the highest performance possible, because only then will we be truly working through the performer.

How Do I Use This Understanding?

This is a good question to which there is no ready answer. This is part of the 'art' of coaching. To assist I offer some of the insights I have gained and the principles by which I have tried to work.

As we learn more about ourselves and other people so we shall also increase the opportunity to unlock and make use of these powerful intrinsic forces for performance improvement. Naturally this has important implications for how we interact with our people, for it is extremely difficult to tell people what their intrinsic motives are. One can only truly find out by involving people through asking them.

Both groups of motives, extrinsic and intrinsic, are valuable and powerful but the coach has control only over the extrinsic factors and even here it may not be total. So what should the coach do about the intrinsic motives that are so strong and long-lasting? Leave their growth to chance? Of course not, the coach can work to influence the intrinsic motives positively and this can be approached along two tracks:

- first, make modifications to the extrinsic motivators that might positively influence the intrinsic

- secondly, influence the intrinsic motives through the way of working with the performers.

Involvement and participation in decision-making promote the shift of energy from 'I have to do it for you' towards 'I want to do it for myself/my team'.

Genuine involvement and participation demand that we fully acknowledge what the performer can offer. This approach is in complete harmony with the generating of awareness and responsibility, the core of high-quality coaching as described in Chapter 4. Involving performers has the potential to generate in them both higher quality input and information (awareness) and better choices from which they may find and own the best ways forward (responsibility).

Conclusion

Extrinsic motivators are often seen as tangible things and so they are, for they have to be something that the performer can see. On the other hand, many of the most powerful intrinsic motivators are less tangible. Perhaps too often because we can see the tangible more than the intangible, we fall into the trap of perceiving the extrinsic as the more important and more powerful than the intrinsic, and yet when we speak to people who have performed outstandingly, say in some physical activity, the sense of personal achievement far outweighs any reward they may have gained as a result of their achievement. While it may be the gold medal that you strive for it is always the sense of achievement that you remember and the feeling of under-achievement that you regret.

We have relied too much upon the extrinsic motivators to promote high performance both in ourselves and in others. This has not necessarily been a result of the way that we have developed people, but it is the result of a combination of factors, such as economic growth, social structure and company structures and processes. It has not been that we have been unaware of the importance of intrinsic motivation, rather that we believed perhaps too strongly in both the power of the extrinsic motivators and of their impact upon intrinsic motivation. Perhaps it is the intrinsic motivation that is central to performance and which then allows the extrinsic motivators to be useful and effective, rather than the other way round. This subtle difference has major implications for the way in which we interact with people and even with ourselves.

High-quality coaching aligned to the generation of tactical, technical, physiological and psychological improvement is essential if the team coach is to harness the greatest motivators of all, those that lie within the performers.

CHAPTER TEN

Generating Feedback and Feed Forward

It has been said that 'feedback is the breakfast of champions'. Without feedback there can be no planned, progressive, performance improvement. It is not that feedback is just more purposeful, it is imperative if performers are to make optimal progress. Within our own internal bodily systems feedback (or on-going monitoring) is the source of the information that influences our next action (feed forward). Feedback and human performance are inseparable: try leaving your performers with no feedback and see what happens.

Blame may be viewed as a form of feedback and one that fails to generate within the performer the levels of honesty, openness, trust and support necessary for the risk-taking inherent with the aspiration to be the best one can. If blame is a poor method with which to provide feedback, it is essential to find a more appropriate one.

The Purpose of Feedback

If feedback is indeed the breakfast of champions, what does it need to provide that is so important in the nourishment of performers and their performance?

Performers require feedback in order to provide:

- an evaluation of performance against set objectives
- a detailed description of what actually took place
- evidence of how much progress has been made
- clarification of the areas where performance is above, equal to and below expectation.
- new learning
- an area within which further development needs to be focused.

If so much valuable information can come from the feedback process it is worth considerable effort to make this as effective as possible. Simply put, the process has to generate clear, accurate details based upon facts that enable the performer to measure his achievement against targets, and to learn and to use that learning for his future performance.

To achieve this we need a process that draws information from all relevant sources and maintains as much objectivity and ownership as possible. In the language of performance coaching, the feedback process needs to yield high levels of awareness and responsibility. Awareness is the gathering of all the relevant feedback information and responsibility is the choosing to own both the learning and the next steps for improvement. Involving all the relevant sources includes the coaches, the performers and any additional information that sources such as video film or computer data might produce. To include all of these, demands and generates a dialogue rather than a monologue. 'Giving' feedback demands and generates only a monologue. It may be only a small change in wording and yet it is a substantial shift in philosophy. 'Generating' acknowledges the process as a dialogue at the outset. This in turn acknowledges an equality in the process; an important acknowledgement if you are the performer. In any case, whose performance is it?

There is an important message here for all coaches: the performance belongs to the performer. Performers have experienced it in minute detail and have probably made many tiny self-corrections in the process. If we can access this knowledge and experience during the feedback process, then we may be able to enhance it even more. Many of the best coaches of elite performers acknowledge that the most powerful and effective feedback sessions are those in which the performers themselves are able to generate detailed and accurate reflections on their own performance. This should never make obsolete the information from all the other sources, yet the coach has no other as close to the action or as sensitive to the performance as the performer. Our challenge is to access this source.

Types of Feedback Process

Table 7 illustrates the several types of feedback we are able to generate. I have added a column that links the feedback to the level of awareness and responsibility it might generate.

Allow me to take you through this procees in some detail to illustrate the importance of generating the most appropriate feedback process.

First, reflect on yourself as the performer having just completed the first match in a tournament. What do you need before the next match in the competition? Yes, reflection on your performance from several important sources, support, the identification of areas of strength and of areas for development, and learning to take to the next match; in short, feedback. And what do almost all performers want to watch early in this process? The video film of it, of course! The reason being that this shows them what happened in an objective manner. It is a description rather than a judgement. Performers seek such a description to help them to evaluate their performance.

In fact, we regularly hear people attempting to learn from the past performance phase by saying, 'We should reserve judgement for a while.' This is a sound point of view that we ignore all too easily and all too often. Notice how quickly people (coaches and performers) slip into judgement:

'That was a poor/great/rubbish/average performance.'
'What a poor/great performer.'

These judgemental statements do not really offer anything of value in the early phases of the generation of feedback and yet we persist in the habit. (Incidentally, remember that a 'habit' could be defined as a response without the appropriate awareness.)

So what might we do to generate a more appropriate feedback process? We could involve the performers by asking them 'How did you play?' or 'How was the match?'.

'I played badly.'
'We were great.'
'The team was terrible', comes the reply.

Damn it! Now they are judging themselves . . . Good intention but a poor question. The vagueness of the question allowed the performers to slip too easily into self-judgement.

Type of Feedback	Content	Level of Awareness and Responsibility Generated
Performer describes own performance/behaviour	Personal description based on their experience, facts and evidence	High
Third party describes the performer's behaviour/ performance	Coach's description based on his observations, video or other data based on facts and what happened	
Performers judge themselves and/or their performance	Judgement (good, bad, etc.) based on rapidly formed opinion, against subjective criteria (sometimes emotionally driven)	
Third party judges the performer's behaviour or performance		
No feedback given	Nothing	Low

Table 7. The Feedback Process

If we want to promote description we have to find questions that focus attention on detail. The video camera provides a detailed description from which the performers can monitor and evaluate their performance. The questions that we ask have to generate the same kind of detail. Examples might include:

- questions that link performance to specific team, group and personal objectives
- questions that focus on specific phases and occurrences in the match
- questions for specific sub-groups to consider
- questions that generate facts rather than opinions (although personal perceptions are unavoidable).

While these questions will generate much more description it is important that the facilitator maintains the focus upon facts and experience rather than on judgement; people can easily and quickly slip into the latter, as we have seen.

The other sources of description (coaches, video film and third parties) may provide their input to the process. If the two sets of descriptions, from the performers and the third parties, are significantly different there then has to be an important discussion. While this may be difficult to handle it at least will be based more upon fact than opinion.

It is my experience that this is the only way to tackle the issues of under-performing players and poor performances successfully. Judgements involve opinions and generate emotional responses however well you may handle them. Description involves facts and behaviour, and while there may be emotional reactions the process itself is less likely to generate them.

Generating description rather than judgement does not guarantee an excellent feedback process every time but it does increase the likelihood of positive outcomes. The process is performer-centred and descriptive yet performance-focused and demanding.

Thorough evaluation of performance against criteria is essential (this might be termed 'judgement'), but it is borne out of marking the performance (description) against our objectives. If in doubt, think of a court of law: judgement is the last phase of the process after all the evidence (description) has been provided. There is nothing wrong with judgement – as a conclusion to our feedback process.

Feedback to Feed Forward

It is a small step to take the quality of information generated in the descriptive feedback process and apply it to the next performance phase. This is the feed forward.

During a match a player who is highly aware will review the situations occurring during performance, extract the key learning and apply it immediately, without the coach's assistance. At a micro level this is high-quality feedback being generated by the performer and applied (feed forward). All coaches should be delighted when they see their performers showing such self-reliance. This is how they need to be if they are to fulfil their potential, but 'players who continually look to the bench for solutions should be on the bench'.

The role of the coach is to generate feedback to such a high level that it provides all the nourishment required by the performers to give them the ability and resourcefulness to achieve even more next time.

Are Harsh Words Wrong?

The simple answer to this is no. There are times when strong, harsh words are necessary. They are exactly what the performers need and that is the essential point. As coaches and leaders we need to say what the performers need to hear, not just what we want to say. The first half of the sentence puts the performers at the centre of the process and that is where we must retain our focus. Sometimes, what we want to say – often emotionally charged – coincides with what they need to hear, but only sometimes.

The way I found out what was best to say was to get into conversation with players and match their thoughts and feelings against mine. Invariably this produced a useful signpost for me, whether it was a pre-match, half-time or post-match intervention.

With regard to the content, the more it is description, based upon facts and behaviour, the more awareness-raising the delivery, and if the harsh words can be drawn out of the performers themselves, the more powerful the whole process. Players in a strong team can often take harsher words from one another than they can take from management.

The Timing of Feedback

When is the most challenging time for any coach to have to do a press conference after a match? Immediately after the performance we say and everyone nods wisely. A press conference or interview is a form of feedback session. What holds us back from encouraging the interview immediately after the conclusion of the match? What causes us to go into press conferences a little late? Primarily our recognition that we want to reflect on things, to allow calmness to be the dominant feeling, to take control of ourselves and the situation. In this way we know that we shall handle the interview more effectively.

Immediately after the performance coaches may have high levels of energy and emotion still centred on the performance or some aspect of it – an incident, the referees, specific players or the disappointments. The dangers of energy and emotion are that they may block 'awareness' and if we want to deliver a press conference or a half-time talk to the highest level then high awareness is essential. Too often coaches and managers live to regret the comments made when awareness was inhibited through energy and emotion; they may be good press but less than effective leadership.

Players face the same issues. At the end of the performance their energy and emotions are locked into the performance they have just experienced. To attempt to cut through this immediately with an objective review will almost certainly meet with blockages. Individuals and teams vary but a cooling-down or period for reflection is essential. The exact timing of the post-match review will depend upon such factors as:

- the time of the next match
- administrative arrangements (such as official functions or travel)
- the stage of the competition
- the importance or status of this match and the next
- the needs of the team and individuals.

The guiding principles, during my work were:

- each match must be reviewed (however briefly) to allow us to leave it and move on
- performer-generated feedback tends to create higher levels of quality information and ownership of ways forward
- post-mortems are not guaranteed to generate high quality feedback; dissecting a corpse is not quite the same as reviewing performance and capturing learning for our next engagement; post-mortems are sombre affairs focusing totally on the past; feedback is a more dynamic process with a strong focus on the future
- feedback must occur before the team energy naturally shifts to the next match
- to ask questions engages awareness and can be used to harness energy and emotion in a positive manner; this is particularly useful in meetings where energy and emotions are high.

Half-time

You have 10 to15 minutes, or even fewer in many sports, to gather people together, relax them, address medical issues such as treatment and re-hydration, and prepare them for the next phase.

This is a daunting task but you do have some excellent helpers: the performers. They know the challenge and they want to succeed. The first thing is organization and structure: have a structure and stick to it. Within this have your own system of achieving the goals you need to achieve for the benefit of the players.

The structure we followed was elementary:

- first phase: 5 minutes: calming down, personal rehydration and medical attention
- second phase: 4 minutes: beginning the refocus; small groups focus with the coach
- final phase: 3 minutes: key messages (no more than about three) to the player
- return to the pitch.

There were variations on this theme according to the situation but the basic pattern remained the same. It was not necessarily the best but it provided the routine within which the detailed work could be done.

My system within this structure was also quite simple:

- during the final few minutes of play in the first half I captured the most significant issues as seen from my (management) perspective
- during first 3 to 4 minutes of half-time speak to most of the players; I asked them questions because this tapped into their energies and emotions about the game, released some of these so that they were more receptive to inputs and gave me insights into what the team needed to hear from me
- where appropriate I would draw two or three players together to address a major issue (or leave them to do it)
- confirm with other management my two or three main points
- involve a player in a public comment if appropriate
- focus attention on the key areas.

In this way I found that I was able to use this short period of time effectively. You will find your own way in your sport and I encourage you to find the most appropriate way for your players.

CHAPTER ELEVEN

Generating Self-Managing and Fast-Forming Teams

Successful, self-managing teams and fast-forming teams are good examples of the spirit of co-operation in action. They are also good vehicles for the exploration and development of important team concepts such as empowerment, leadership, authority, accountability, performance goals and the establishment of ways of working together.

The desire to have teams that are able to self-manage themselves and to form and re-form rapidly is borne out of the need to develop performers who are capable of dealing with the dynamic situation on the pitch. It is encapsulated in the remark quoted in the last chapter that 'players who continually look to the bench for the solutions might as well be on the bench'.

The process of generating teams capable of self-management and of being fast-forming and re-forming would also promote higher levels of co-operation within the team. We do not have to wait for the co-operative qualities to be developed before we can explore self-management and fast-forming and re-forming. They can be mutually enhancing.

The gains for the team are many. The process enables the team members to:

- recognize and understand the key factors upon which decisions are made

- take the leadership and allow it to shift appropriately among players

- take responsibility and authority for key decisions

- experience and develop mutual accountability for the outcomes of their actions

- experience and understand the power of establishing and following through agreed ways of working together.

All of these would be represented in any list of the qualities of a highly co-operative team.

Self-Managing Teams

What is the purpose?

To enable the team or sub-team to take much greater control of the decision-making and to enable better responses to be made to the changing circumstances within the game.

How is it done?

The easiest process is to begin with small sections of play such as set pieces (such as free kicks, corners or restarts) or by calling a kind of tactic in response to certain cues (as after scoring, before a formal break in play, or when the opposition make an error or play in a specific way).

To enable the team to make the most appropriate decision they have to be aware of:

- the cues from the opposition and what these mean
- the roles and responsibilities of their own players
- contingency plans to cover errors and the unforeseen
- the detail of the variations available to them
- the parameters within which they have authority.

The best process in my experience of generating the abilities to self-manage involved:

- the detailed participation of the performers in all stages of the process through meetings of the full team or squad and the appropriate sub-teams
- the establishment of clear purpose and performance goals within the area of work
- the collection of all the relevant information from video film, personal observation, previous experience and discussions
- communication of the details to the appropriate people and agreement on roles and responsibilities
- the assessment of the data, the development of our responses and possible solutions and agreement on actions
- putting into operation on the practice ground and in competition, and continually reviewing progress.

The process followed the principles of high-quality coaching described in Chapters 4 and 5. The purpose was to involve the performers in generating high levels of awareness and responsibility such that they took real ownership of the agreed solutions.

Within the post-performance review the performers also learned to accept mutual accountability for their decisions and the execution of agreed plans. This in turn offered improvements in the whole process for the next time. This enhances co-operation and allows the performers to take the power at the appropriate times.

How far can you go?

The simple answer is: 'As far as you want to go.' However, circumstances and feasibility will limit you. One important point is not to allow yourself to limit the degree of self-management because of the authority that you feel it may take away from you. This is perception rather than reality. The generating of empowerment does not reduce your position of leadership or authority.

Fast-Forming and Re-Forming Teams

What is the purpose?

To generate the teamwork to such a level that the changing of the personnel has no adverse effect upon team progress and to allow sub-teams to work more effectively within the fast moving dynamics of the competitive or pressured arena.

How is it done?

While the fast-forming teams themselves may differ considerably from one another, the principles behind their formulation are the same. For each of them there may be a different emphasis upon certain factors according to the unique needs or functions of the team but all the factors have to be addressed.

In hockey, while there is a squad of sixteen players available with eleven of them on the pitch at any one time, the reality is that in many circumstances the game consists of a series of rapidly forming and re-forming smaller teams. The best teams not only enable this to happen but also actively work to make sure that it can happen successfully no matter which players make up the sub-teams. These sub-teams may be accomplishing one of many tactical situations, such as:

- a fast counterattack
- a set move in open play
- a planned restart
- the pressuring of an opponent in possession
- the pressuring of an area of the pitch in which the ball is trapped
- the defence against a fast counterattack.

The most important questions that need to be addressed are:

- what is the purpose of the sub-team in this situation?
- what specific goals within our control are the team and its individual members focusing upon?
- how shall we use our skills/talents/abilities in a complementary way?
- what are the key principles that underpin the way we work together in this situation?

Again the need is to involve the performers in this process of raising their awareness of all the relevant details and principles and agreeing upon the ways forward. The main elements of the process were set out above.

A Worked Example

When the British men's hockey team won the Olympic gold medal in Seoul in 1988 the views of the other coaches could be summed up as 'Great Britain did not appear to have the best individuals, but easily had the best team'. We had three or four world-class players within the team, yet our opponents saw the teamwork as so good that the individuals did not readily stand out.

What had we done? Put simply, we had established values, rules and patterns of play which we agreed with and which we practised in the way we worked together. Through this process the team understanding and trust within our working and performing environment grew to a high level – one that unlocked the door to exceptional performance.

The growth took time, yet it enabled the team and its sub-teams to form and re-form at speed more quickly than it had ever done before: an apparent paradox of taking time to save time. The best teams in sport and in other aspects of life successfully form and re-form at speed. What is it that they do to achieve this and what is the learning here for all teams?

Within the game, small teams are continually forming and re-forming as the ball moves around the pitch. People come together to work in harmony to achieve an immediate objective, but one that supports the match objectives. They need one another's co-operation to succeed and the better their teamwork the greater is the likelihood of the team's success. The concept of 'total soccer' or 'fifteen-man rugby' is built upon these small teams forming and re-forming so effectively that it rarely matters which individuals are involved. Forwards can play as backs and vice versa. This happens in modern rugby, soccer and hockey and we delight in the results of it.

The ability to form and re-form rapidly is built on an understanding of what is required in various situations and positions and the players' capabilities to perform what is required; the awareness of the situation and the responsibility to act appropriately during the 'heat of battle' is central to continual improvements in performance and continued success.

In order to explore what is required in high-quality teamwork let us use a different game: bridge.

The objective in bridge is quite simple: through a structured, verbal bidding process the two pairs of players in competition attempt to inform one another of the strength of their hands and one pair wins the right to attempt an agreed contract. In the second phase of the game the cards are played with one side seeking to 'beat' the other. In both phases there are clear procedures that govern play. These allow people to come together to play the game. If a new pair or team follows these it can achieve some teamworking, but it would probably not initially be of a very high quality.

Within bridge there are conventions of play that allow pairs to operate at a more sophisticated level. These conventions are agreements about how to respond in various situations within the game. They allow the pairs to go to a more detailed level in both the bidding and the playing of the cards (increased awareness) and increase the likelihood of better team-work (better responses).

At an even more detailed level a pair that plays regularly together may develop even more subtle variations within their agreed style of playing that enhance their teamwork still further. This level of awareness will grow out of the discussions they have both around and within their perfor-mance. The team cannot attain this level of teamworking without having team communication of high quality.

If I transfer these rules, conventions and local variations to sporting teams I find many parallels. For these the rules are probably clearly under-stood because they are rules of the game. They will provide an excellent foundation for teamworking in the game. However, there also need to be some rules for how the team works together away from the game. If these are missing the quality of the teamwork in training, preparation and review may be impaired.

Beneath this important, yet superficial, level of 'rules' sporting teams have ways of playing. They have their equivalent of 'conventions'. These will, of course, manifest themselves in many ways, including team forma-tions (such as 4-2-4 or 2-4-4), types of defence (such as half court, full press, man-to-man or sliding) and styles of play (for instance, fast break, long ball, ten-man rugby or counterattack). Within these conventions clear roles and responsibilities are established and, provided that everyone is clear as to what is required, an interchange of personnel does not adversely affect team performance.

However, in reality teams may play to the same convention yet perform in a significantly different manner to one another. These differences are the result of exploring the next level of team interaction, the 'local variations'. Within this level the focus is upon understanding and having access to the unique talents and ways of working found within the team members. Particular strengths of certain players may allow variations upon a 'convention' that significantly enhance team effectiveness, such as the power, pace, technical brilliance or tactical awareness of one individual. Within agreed patterns of play each will have his own way of doing things (moving, giving and receiving a pass, for instance) and the more each player is in tune with the unique ways of other players with whom they interact the greater the opportunity for high-quality teamwork. This level of teamwork can only be achieved through high-quality coaching and the performers' taking real responsibility.

There is no short cut to high-quality teamwork and this book is focused upon generating the environment and interaction that opens up that level of teamworking, drawing upon the unique abilities and variations that lie within the performers. Nevertheless, it is essential to have the 'rules' and 'conventions' levels as the foundations.

Through studying how sub-teams form and re-form quickly, I found much that could be applied to other teams. If you had to put a team together quickly – a playing or a management team – upon which levels would you invest your time and for what reasons? What factors would cause you to alter this emphasis?

Finally, let us return to an example of teamwork away from sport. How is it that outstanding musicians can come together and harmonize in an unrehearsed session, or actors improvise so well, or players exhibit excellent teamwork with no rehearsal? Because they know the rules, conventions and detail so well, and recognize the cues so quickly that their responses sustain high-quality teamwork. What if we could enable our players to learn these things more quickly?

How Far Can You Go?

This process may be used for management teams and all its sub-teams (medical, video and match analysis) as well as for the playing team.

It is a natural extension of the teamworking done every training day with teams but it gives extra focus. If the goal is to have performers who are capable of continually forming and re-forming highly effective sub-teams during play, then everyone must understand both the principles and the processes. Doing this demands and generates co-operative practices within the team and positively contributes to 'spirit'.

What Do These Processes Demand of the Leader?

Coaches cannot tread this path successfully unless they are willing to:

- acknowledge and respect the knowledge and views of the performers
- truly involve them in decision-making
- allow leadership to shift to and between the performers
- support the inevitable risk-taking inherent in the decisions by the performers
- let go of the power of decision-making at appropriate times
- model the principles they are trying to promote in their performers
- properly explore with their performers the principles that underpin success in a wide range of situations within the competitive area
- recognize that they may not know all the detail themselves
- follow and learn in the wake of their performers.

CHAPTER TWELVE

Selection and Deselection

'Selecting the best team does not mean selecting the best players.'

Selection and Team 'Spirit'

Generating this intangible 'spirit' in a team begins when the squad first comes together. It is not something a coach can leave until after the selection process is complete. Having said this, selection does have an impact upon the growth of team spirit and coaches would be wise to recognize its potential effects and make allowances for and take advantage of the situation.

Every squad has critical selection points within its life cycle and it is all too easy for coaches and managers to forget or be unaware of the pressures upon players and relationships for the simple reason that the coach and the manager are already selected.

As the selection point approaches players may easily slip into behaviour and an energy focus associated with the 'assertion' phase of team development. In their desire to be selected they become focused on only their personal performance and on promoting themselves above others. The supporting of other members may often be forgotten and self-preservation become evident. This rather extreme picture is unlikely to occur regularly but it is offered merely to illustrate the point. It would be quite natural for there to be subtle shifts to a more self-centred and self-interested approach. If coaches are aware of this then they can cater for it.

First, it may be an excellent opportunity to restate the prime selection criteria, and high-quality teamwork may be one of them. Secondly, if the shifts in the behaviour and the energy of a player are marked during this pressurized period then these might be important indications of how that player is likely to react under tournament pressure. This cannot be certain, but it is all part of the information that coaches and managers have to take into consideration when building a team that has all the core requirements, including the spirit to win.

After the selection point has passed there is always a surge in positive energy within those that are continuing. This may be the final competition or tournament squad or merely a stepping stone towards this point. This increase in positive energy offers an opportunity for coaches to harness it for the benefit of the spirit within the team or squad. There are any number of vehicles a coach can create to use and build on this energy but it needs to be:

- appropriate and relevant for the situation and squad
- positively focused or orientated
- promoting co-operative qualities
- involving all the team or squad
- adding value to team development.

There are times when a selection issue results in a lowering of energy and enthusiasm within a squad. This might occur when a senior or core player withdraws unexpectedly through injury, illness or retirement. The challenge now is rather different. The situation is clear and unexpected, so how can it be used to our advantage? The need in the squad is to find ways to cover the gap left and to reverse the negative energies. My experience is that these situations are best dealt with quickly through the involvement of the whole squad in some manner.

We lost two key players at an Olympic qualifying tournament after the deadline for nominated players had passed. We selected from fourteen players (including two goalkeepers) for over half the tournament. We involved all the squad in the problem and the solution, to the benefit of everyone and the team (we qualified easily).

This leads to the next type of selection issue for a team: those within the tournament or competition arena. The whole squad is present but only a certain number represent it in the match or at the start. The rules of each sport or competition regarding the time of team nomination and substitutions will have an important bearing upon when selections are made and how they are communicated to the squad. In addition there is the impact of the selection upon individual players, sub-groups within the squad, such as players sharing a room, and the squad as a whole.

There are so many possible 'issues' that may arise in these situations as to make it impossible to account for them all. I offer some basic questions I have used as guidelines:

- does the selection generate any special issues that need attention?
- should any individual be informed privately?
- does the selection show a pattern of selection that may be sending messages that require clarification? (for example: is one player starting on the bench yet again? Is a 'first-team' team emerging?)
- what social stresses (room relationships) does this selection generate?
- when is the best time to inform the performers of the selection?
- how is it best to inform them?
- what processes will we use to 'include' those who are not starting?

The selection process, because it is in the hands of management and because it is by nature inclusive–exclusive, has the potential to affect adversely the spirit within the team. Coaches and managers can minimize the dangers and maximize the gains of the selection process provided that they become fully aware of the effects of the selection process, work in accordance with clear principles and establish an agreed selection process. This section has explored the first of these.

The Principles and Process of Selection

Once again it is impossible to draw up a set of principles that are applicable to all teams in all situations. Each coach has to address this key area for himself and his own sport. What I suggest below are some of the principles I have tried to follow and some of the questions I have posed to myself to clarify the details of the process.

The selection criteria should be stated clearly:

- What are the core selection criteria?
- What are the criteria of highest priority?
- Does this priority alter as the squad is reduced towards the competition size (for instance, the ability to work well as a team member may replace personal specialism as a priority)?
- Are there any inconsistencies between theory and application (for instance, performance is given high priority over fitness and yet only the fittest get selected)?

These criteria should be available to performers and others, where appropriate:

- How much detail do they want or need?
- What targets can be given a minimal expectation?
- When should they have the criteria?
- Who else should have access to these criteria?

Performers should be given equal opportunity to demonstrate their abilities:

- How 'equal' can this be in reality?
- What can be done to make opportunity as fair as possible?
- How do we define equal?
- What abilities do the performers want to show (for instance, to offer an alternative role or specialist skills)?

Performers have the right to personal feedback when they are the subject of deselection:

- How is this best achieved?
- How will the process differ at different times in the life-cycle of the squad?
- Selection is solely based upon the agreed criteria and excludes any personal feelings towards individual performers.

Information related to selection will be drawn from agreed sources in addition to the coach:

- What information is required for effective selection?
- Who and what are the most appropriate sources?
- Who do the players agree are the appropriate sources?
- How will the information be gathered?

Information related to selection must remain confidential within an agreed group and the performers must know of this group:

- Who will have access to this information?
- When will players know who knows of this information?
- How will confidentiality be ensured?

The selection procedures and timescales must be clearly identified and communicated to performers and other relevant personnel:

- When are the critical selection points?
- What is the best way in which to inform players of selection?
- Who is the appropriate person to inform the players?
- How and when is it best communicated to non-selected players?
- How will be the feedback to non-selected and deselected players be managed?
- How will other appropriate personnel be informed?
- What will be said to the media, when and by whom?

Prima Donnas

Almost as a postscript I offer some thoughts on highly talented yet difficult performers in the team setting. These performers are often challenging to coaches and managers because they do not easily conform to the team norms during competition or outside it.

The easiest solution for management is not to have them in a squad or team, but that is probably not the best way forward for the team. Ideally the management team would like this wayward talent to conform to normal team behaviour, as the majority of performers willingly do. There may be some core agreements that are sacrosanct and which must be adhered to by all performers if they are to be members of the squad or team. These are likely to be small in number and central to the group's values.

Unfortunately for coaches and managers, the prima donnas rarely choose to conform to structures and obviously it has been their individuality that has made them stand out in the first place. The retaining of this uniqueness may become a strong driving force within this performer, even fighting against sensible team norms for space. This may pose a real dilemma for management.

Experience and observation show that, provided that the performer delivers high-quality performance to the team, it can and will be willing to handle many of the other issues both within and around the competitive environment. However, when the performer no longer contributes that additional value to the team the rest are likely to be unwilling to provide the extra support and the 'issues' come to the surface.

The real skill of coaches and managers with highly talented yet difficult performers is to watch carefully both the performance of the prima donna and the tolerance level in the rest of the team. Action must be taken before either of these indicators reaches danger point.

CHAPTER THIRTEEN

Tournament Issues and Team Spirit

If tournaments were just about playing then they would be so much easier. The challenges of how the quality of individual and team performance influences the spirit of the team are obviously a core part of the work of a management team. However, there is another set of variables that may have subtle yet powerful influences upon the team and the spirit within it. These include the behaviour of the management team, friends and family, and the media, the roomings and life within the tournament environment.

Early Successes and Disappointments

It is self-evident that early successes generate positive energies within a team. This may be a team success or an individual achievement used to promote greater team morale. While 'winning' early in a tournament cannot be guaranteed, good goal setting can provide the opportunity for a range of smaller successes all of which can contribute to team spirit. All these have to be put into a realistic context otherwise it becomes a 'game' of always finding the positive. If the unpopular truth is that the team should have won then it has to be so acknowledged. This does not detract from some positive outcomes but to ignore it because it is uncomfortable is dangerous. The realization of the disappointment can be used as motivation.

Poor Performances

Everyone's intention, desire and focus is to perform to the highest possible level, but there are times when teams perform poorly by their own standards. It may be hoped that this need not inhibit success in the tournament as a whole. Winning while playing well below their best is quite common with some very successful teams. The key is to improve as the tougher stages of the tournament approach. This pattern is not uncharacteristic and the normal processes of generating feedback and of modifying the playing objectives apply.

Unfortunately, there are times when both the performance and the results are poor. In these cases some simple principles can apply both to the team and individuals:

- the truth supported by evidence is essential
- we are all in this, both players and management, and mutual accountability has to be accepted
- focus upon factors that are within the squad's (or the player's) control
- reassess the goals both for the next match and the tournament, and revise if appropriate
- involve the players in this process
- establish commitment to any revised plans
- avoid blame and retribution, they are entry points to a downward spiral for spirit and performance.

A 'First' Team

Having such a team is almost unavoidable with a squad and it should not be avoided if it is the right process for the squad and the sport. The main challenge is to manage the potential problems. These include:

- how do we deal with the competition between players to be in the 'first' team, or 'starting' line-up during the tournament?
- how do we retain the focus of the 'substitutes' in team preparation?
- how can we best prepare players who enter the game rather than begin the game?
- how do we 'exercise' these substitutes if they do not play, for they inevitably build up adrenaline?
- how can we positively include those who have not played within a purposeful review session?

The answer to these questions for your team lie within you and your performers. I encourage you to find the key questions and to discover the answers for they are important to the spirit of your team. In addition, consider how much you might be able to prepare for this before the tournament, competition or tour.

For myself, I did find that I arrived at a 'starting' team in all the major tournaments. I preferred the advantages we gained from this stability and worked to minimize the obvious disadvantages.

Friends and Family

The partners and family of the performers are extremely important people. They have probably given the greatest level of support to the performer, over and above anything the team management could provide. However, their appearance at competitions may be a double-edged sword. On the positive side they can provide:

- extra emotional, physical and psychological support
- a social outlet for the tensions of competition.

On the debit side these relationships may:

- distract the attention of the performer
- put inappropriate pressures on him
- cut across the team development process
- show a lack of awareness of the importance of intra-team relationships during competition
- be over-supportive and protective to the unintentional detriment of other team members.

The challenge must be to promote and use the positive contributions that such people can offer to the performers' success. To handle the friends and family group you might:

- describe the potential advantages and problems to them
- involve them and value their contributions before and during the tournament
- make it fair for those performers who do not have friends or family present.

Including this group and structuring its inclusion allows it to be in the control of the management with a greater chance of positive outcomes.

Media

The media have a simple purpose and objective. The purpose is to contribute to their own commercial success and the objective is therefore to find stories that will contribute to it. The sport wants to have media coverage that enhances its own image such that it can attract public support, more performers and higher sponsorship income. It is hardly surprising that the relationship between sport and the media is sometimes strained.

The skill of coaches and managers in handling the media is increasingly important and while there are many aspects to it the focus here is on generating team spirit. From my experience in a successful amateur sport in the Olympic arena I would offer the following insights:

- keep all interactions with the media as much within your own control as possible
- agree on the procedures and the reasons for them with your performers
- direct all media requests to a central person
- share out the interviews among the players; this may necessitate providing the 'story line' to a particular paper
- avoid public criticism of players by management
- show courtesy and respect and yet be firm and guarded
- understand the media's role but think only of what is best for the team.

The media and their reports have the power to undermine or to enhance the spirit of the team; used wisely they may enhance, used foolishly they may destroy.

Management Behaviour

The management team should adhere to the same rules and behaviour as the team or to a set that have been agreed with it. The management team will also have specific roles and responsibilities related to leading and supporting the performers in their quest for high achievement.

The manner in which the management team behave and fulfil their responsibilities has a distinct bearing upon both the relationships between the management and the performers and the whole culture of the squad. To promote a culture characterized by high professional behaviour, openness, integrity and supportiveness demands that the management models these in everything it does: 'Do as I say rather than as I do' is not a leadership style associated with sustained high performance.

What are your management agreements?
What are the roles and responsibilities?
What are your agreed working practices?
How regularly will you monitor the quality of your working together?

Having the answers to these questions will not only enhance your teamwork but also provide important support to the culture of co-operation within the squad. The added value to the 'spirit' may appear small but it is significant when the team is looking for the 'edge' in tight competition.

The management team is one in its own right and should give time to the establishing of:

- the purpose of this team
- the performance goals for the individuals, sub-groups and the team as a whole
- the skills it possesses and how these complement one another
- the way in which the team agrees to work together.

While all these areas are important the last is perhaps the most critical within the tournament arena as everyone will be working under intense pressure at some point. Recognition of how each member responds in these situations and the provision of the appropriate support can do much to minimize any adverse effects on relationships and the team spirit. Meet regularly, have clear agendas and focus upon both the discussion and how well everyone is working together.

My preference was to have times fixed for team management meetings a couple of days ahead so that everyone knew what was happening. At these meetings each section – administration, injury, illness and health – was given time for reporting and discussions along with other issues as they arose. Care and attention to detail is as important within the team management as it is between management and performers.

Social Groupings

In larger squads social sub-groups occur naturally. These can be helpful for the team and provide natural outlets for it and its energies and also interest during rest and relaxation. It may be important to take these social groupings into account when making room allocations. Within competitions, players have to live together for a considerable time so compatibility is important. Nothing has the potential to erode team spirit more rapidly than disharmony between people who have to live together.

Some questions may assist in this important yet sensitive area:

- how much can you involve the players in the process?
- what information would you like to have?
- who is best to collect this information?
- who else should be involved?
- how much can you prepare the players before the competition?

When coupled with a good set of rules for behaviour on both competition days and rest days, drawn up by the players, the answers to these should provide a sound foundation for group relationships that enhance team spirit.

Meetings . . . Bloody Meetings

Outside of matches and training the most common form of team interaction takes the form of meetings. They are far more than a convenient and efficient medium for communicating information. They provide further opportunity for dynamic interaction between team members and a forum in which many issues can be discussed, explored and resolved. They are a key vehicle for promoting and generating the processes that contribute to the important concept of spirit in the team.

If your aspirations are to build a high-performing team capable of taking real responsibility in the environment of competition then team meetings must contribute to this process; they must reflect the desire to promote high levels of co-operation, learning and responsibility through the process of involving the performers deeply in the development and growth of the team. This demands that the coach uses the same processes to promote an environment of empowerment within meetings for the reason that they are an integral part of training and competition.

Meetings demand as much planning as training and competition for they are part of these processes. Within tournaments it may be necessary to plan a series of meetings, particularly in the pre-competition phase, because there is so much to cover. Experience suggests that the following areas are worthy of consideration in order to give coaches every opportunity to hold successful team meetings.

The Purpose of the Meeting

Take care to be clear about the purpose of the meeting and what needs to be achieved by the end of it as these factors greatly influence both who should attend and how it is structured. It is dangerous to have too many topics within a meeting since this can split the focus of the performers, causing a loss of emphasis and learning. If it is necessary to have more than one major topic make certain that the most important one is given the appropriate priority with regard to time and position within the agenda.

The questions might be:

- what is the purpose of the meeting?
- what topics need to be covered?
- how relevant is each of these?
- which are the best items to include?
- which are the most important?
- who needs to know the purpose of the meeting?
- who should attend?

Structure of the Meeting

How long should the meeting be? Recognize that energies can diminish rapidly during certain periods of the day and when work loads have been heavy. Keeping meetings to a maximum of an hour is good practice.

Link the purpose of the meeting to the time of day. The more important the the discussion is likely to be, the more important it is that the meeting should be placed at a time when energy levels are likely to be high rather than low. Meetings after participants have travelled across several time zones and before they are accustomed to change require particular care.

> How is it best to structure or organize the meeting to achieve the objectives?
>
> How will the topic be introduced and by whom? If the ideas and possible solutions of the performers are important then it might be counterproductive for the management to put their ideas in too early as this could stifle the performers' creativity.
>
> What are the roles and responsibilities of people within the meeting, such as the coaches, management, senior performers and the captain?
>
> What would be the most productive format for the meeting?
>
> What small group discussions would be useful?
>
> What would be the most useful structure of these groups?
>
> What other factors (objectives) influence the people chosen for each group?
>
> When would they go into groups, for how long and how will their views be shared?
>
> How can the less gregarious be encouraged to contribute publicly?

The needs of the performers also influence the structure and content of the meeting. Final team preparation is primarily coach-led and is highly focused upon restating and emphasizing agreed strategies, tactics, roles and responsibilities. This is what the performers need at this time.

The Content of the Meeting

This often has a bearing on its structure. When the topic is more about information-giving, organization and administration the more likely it is to be done in a directive style. The structure should be short and highly focused.

When the exploration of specific topics in order to generate a range of solutions and find the best ways forward is the purpose, then a more facilitative type is more appropriate. This might involve one or a number of group discussion techniques or processes. The more of these that are available to the coach the more versatile the process can be.

The Environment

The environment of the meeting may influence the tone of the interaction. The environment is influenced by the location, the lay-out and style of the chairs, the lighting and the way in which the meeting is led.

Small areas generate intimacy and yet may be claustrophobic. Public areas and large windows create distractions. Theatre-style chair arrangements are acceptable for receiving information but the structure does not promote eye contact or discussion. Circles are the most natural format for focus, discussion and contact.

The intensity of the lighting may influence the mood of the meeting, with brighter lights bringing formality and more subtle lighting generating greater relaxation. Finally, the style of leadership has a significant effect upon the environment and therefore the tone of the interaction.

The net result is that coaches have a variety of variables at their disposal with which to influence the environment of the meeting. Rarely will we be provided with the perfect setting for our meetings and generating the most appropriate one will depend upon our manipulation of the variables available to us. Take extra care in getting the environment as close to the ideal for the meeting since the benefits may be considerable.

Meetings – for Whom and for What?

Here are some examples to assist in the application of this section to your team.

Meetings might involve:

- the whole team or squad
- sub-teams within the team or squad such as:
  set-piece teams
  an offence/defence
  forwards/backs
  small units that play close together
  captain and vice-captain
- players only
- one-to-one with coach
- the management team
- a sub-group of the management team.

The most common purposes of meetings include:

- administration
- goal-setting for a campaign
- programme planning
- exploring team strategies
- tactical development
- performance review
- competition goal-setting
- team rules and behaviour
- performance expectations of management team
- sharing experience in preparation for competition
- team development (that is, focus on the process of developing co-operation)
- player education (physiology, psychology, nutrition, etc.)
- understanding the opponents
- match briefing (on, for instance, strategy or tactics)
- motivation
- tournaments:
  setting the scene
  what if?
  updates
  administration
- selection
- discipline
- half-time/during competition
- coping with adversity, challenges and problems
- match debriefs.

These are in no order of priority here nor are they comprehensive. These topics might be approached through one or more of the types of group described above (such as the whole squad or team, or sub-teams). To formulate the best process to achieve the prime purpose of any meeting it is essential to consider each of the areas suggested in this section.

CHAPTER FOURTEEN

Case Studies

The two case studies making up this chapter are about teams that achieved outstanding success over a sustained period of time. The stories are told in the words of the leaders themselves, responding to questions I put to them in interview. The text can only provide a flavour of what they did to achieve sustained success, but I hope they will provide the reader with insights to the principles that supported the work of two world-class team coaches.

England Rugby 1987–94

Geoff Cooke was the manager of the England Rugby Union team from October 1987 to April 1994. During that period he led England in forty-nine major international matches, including two tours to Australia/Fiji and one to Argentina. England achieved unparalleled success during this period, including two successive Grand Slams (1991 and 1992) and reaching the final of the World Cup in 1991. Many people recognize that Geoff was responsible for a great change in both the attitudes and the performances of elite players in English rugby. The professionalism that he promoted within the elite squads preceded the professional era of the late 1990s. In 1997 he returned to elite rugby at Bedford RFC, guiding them to the Premier League in his first two seasons.

How did you see your role as a Manager with regard to the development of the team?

Traditionally in English rugby, the team had been managed, if you like, by a Selection Committee of between five and nine people, and a Chairman of Selectors. They picked the team and then they had a Coach who was involved in that process, but perhaps did not have a vote. I always felt that that, in itself, was too unwieldly and for a few years before at different levels I had been working with a much tighter structure: a three-man team. When the opportunity to take over the England side arrived, I said that's how I wanted to do it. In other words, with myself having virtually full responsibility. You know – 'The buck stops here', and I think that's fundamental. The first thing is, you can't run a team by committee. So that was important and if I was going to be held accountable, I wanted the overall responsibility. So when I went in I saw myself as manager/coach in terms of the overall technical development and understanding of the team. I was really the director of operations and I had two people with me, one a very experienced former player and coach, Roger Uttley, and the other a very experienced former player – never played for England but well respected and had been part of the previous set-up – John Elliott. We ran it between the three of us. It was very much a very tight little management team to start with.

How did changing the structure assist in the development of the team?

Basically because it enabled us to ensure that as a group we were speaking with one voice. There was no confusion in the players' minds about what was expected of them and to whom they were accountable. It meant that when we went out to practice, the practices had all been talked through with the three of us beforehand. We were also agreed on exactly what we were trying to achieve when it came to selection, which is a critical part of any team, because if you don't get the people right you're in trouble. It was much easier to get unanimity on what we were looking for with three people doing it – and I always had the final say if it came to that – than if you've got a committee doing it. The key to success, put very simply, is about knowing what you want to achieve, making sure you choose the right people, understanding what is necessary to achieve that success, and putting people in place who you think have got half a chance of making it happen.

What were you looking for in the players in order to get this successful team?

I don't think we knew at first, to be honest, but what we did know was that we felt that, considering the strength of our playing population, we were under-achieving. It was a question of taking what was there to start with and painting a picture of what we thought was possible, and what we thought the team should be achieving with a playing population five times greater than the opponents we were playing against. And then very simply just building confidence. At first we probably overlooked some of the technical deficiencies and just concentrated on the psychology. The reason for this is that you usually go into any new team situation with an inheritance factor, and you cannot just wipe the slate clean. You usually take over an existing team. It is very rare that you start with a completely blank sheet of paper. Somebody's been there before with a different management style and different coaching processes.

What did you feel you offered as a management team to the team that had not been very successful? One you said was confidence, what were the other things?

I think a different perspective and a much more professional approach to the whole business. I've always aspired to be a sport professional/coaching professional, and with all respect to the people that had gone before me, they were amateurs in the development of sporting teams. They were people who operated at a high level in business, but weren't what I call sports professionals. I set out straight away to apply what I considered to be a professional approach to the preparation of the England rugby team, painting a picture first of what we thought was possible and then enabling the players to believe that they had the ability to get there. They were clearly the best there are in the country, or amongst the best in the country, and by implication they should be among the best in the world, and yet they were not going out and playing like that. I think we also brought in a lot more stability and continuity to the organization.

We approached selection as a critical exercise for ourselves as a management team in that we recognized that if we changed the team after just one game, we were the ones that had made the mistake, not the players. Players are going to make mistakes on the international field, but if we had to continually change the team, we had made a fundamental error in selection. On investigation, I found that the people selecting the teams had been in the habit of selecting on very flimsy evidence. 'Well you had a bad game, so let's give so and so a try.' Or you get a report from someone saying 'Oh, he had a good game last week, so I'm playing him.' Well what do you mean 'had a good game'? What did he do that caused you to come to that conclusion? What did he bring to the team? What was his value to the side? What was effective? I believe we changed the whole way that we looked at players. We explained the reasons we were putting them in the team and what we expected of them, and then added 'Look, we've now picked you because we feel that you are best for the job and we are going to give you a good run at it.'

Were the players aware that that was how you were doing it?

We made them aware of that very clearly. We said 'This is our commitment to you. We're going to try and give stability. We are going to believe in you and help you, but you've got to go out and do it.'

In what way did you feel that that helped with the growth of the team into a high-performing team?

Initially it was a whole new world for these players. They had not been used to that. They had been used to what I call the 'fear factor'. They knew it as the motivator if you like, this very simplistic view that if they were threatened with losing their place in the team, they would go out and play well, whereas in my view the reverse is usually the case. They went onto the field so inhibited, frightened of making mistakes and looking over their shoulder, that they didn't do anything, because they wanted to stay there. It is nice being an England player, you get all the accolades that go with it, and 'if I don't put my head over the parapet I won't get it shot off'. The result was that nothing happened and they became riddled with insecurity about whether they were going to be in the team next week, never knowing that anyone had real confidence or belief in them. I think our approach was a dramatic change for the players. They couldn't believe it at first and were very reluctant to open up and communicate. They were used to being told what to do. Previously they had gone into a team meeting and waited to be told what to do. Now they were being asked their views and included in the preparation and planning. How are we going to beat them? What do they do? What's it like out there? What's it going to be like? What are we going to have to concentrate on? At first they looked at me as if to say; 'Well, you're the bloody coach, isn't it your job to tell us?'.

So the result was a huge cultural shift and changed attitude, and it all came, I think, from trying to give the squad this stability, trying to establish mutual trust and inter-dependency between everyone. Showing we were there to be part of the team, in a different role, but we could not tell them exactly what to do. I mean Roger Uttley could say what they used to do when he played, but that was ten or twelve years go. How much relevance did that have? We managed to start teasing that out, I suppose, eventually. I think building confidence, overcoming the fear of failure, getting them prepared to contribute to the tactical side of things all contributed to a feeling of 'Hang on, wait a minute, somebody actually thinks I have got some ability here and respects me and trusts me to go out and give it my best shot.'

Afterwards we would discuss mistakes and we tried very early on to develop a 'no blame' culture. We promoted collective responsibility and as you get to know people and as you establish that collective responsibility, you are able to criticize their performance in public (within the team environment). I have never really sat easily with the approach of 'praise in public and criticize in private'. International sport is a tough arena and people have to be able to face up to the quality of their performance. As long as the mutual respect is there within the team, the players can handle feedback in a variety of ways.

Another area of major change was within the physical and technical department of the game. We asked them to think of themselves as athletes first and rugby players second. That was a very important shift if they were going to be successful against the best in the world.

How did you promote mutual accountability and in particular the ownership of preparing themselves as athletes?

The ownership of the fitness side was a little bit difficult because there was quite a bit of suspicion at first about what we were trying to do. There was the usual stuff trotted out, that they had jobs and they could only do so much. We brought in athletics coaches and we exposed the players to the training regimes of athletics. We exposed them to other sportspeople and made them understand what other people do. I remember illustrating to them that the average jogger committed to more training than they did. I outlined the sort of work that a person preparing to do a half marathon would be doing. I talked about swimmers that I'd had contact with in my previous experience, the getting up at 5am, doing their training and then going back to school or work. All these people did this and they fitted it into their lifestyle. Then it was a question of asking whether they wanted success, and if they did then only they could do the training and they had to be prepared to work for it. They started to think that it would be better to be well thought-of instead of being constant underachievers, and we provided the support for them to do the training. Initially it was as much education and application. We had to help them to understand that it was not a question of going out and doing thousands of miles of running and being physically sick, but of the quality of training. We provided personal fitness counselling and programme design, introduced physiological testing and tried to say that it was not a selection mechanism but a way to help them get the best out of their performance on the field. It was a very slow, painful process, I have to say, for the first two years, but it was worth it. At one stage they were exposed to women athletes who could shift more weight than some of our famous forwards! That had never been done before: they had never ever been exposed to that type of approach. They had never been properly challenged in this area.

In addition no one had done any personal counselling with them with regard to their playing strengths and weaknesses, and how training and development programmes might help them. The previous regimes had never really generated any accountability for their own actions on the field, so when they came off the field after a bad game they'd blame anything, everybody. All our interactions were designed to change this.

How did you find that you used your team meetings? What was the subject of them? How were they run? What different structures did you use?

It varied according to the location, the time of year, the proximity to a big game. If we were away on tour, team meetings took on a different perspective because we were together for a much longer period of time. Some of the team meetings would be used for 'basic education'. These might include basic education sessions on why this type of fitness, why be efficient, why psychology, how to concentrate, what it means to set your own goals etc. So if we had the time and it was away from competition, we would use them for that sort of purpose.

One of the most important things we did in team meetings was to actually talk about what is effective, what is winning rugby, and to try to cut through some of the myths about how the game is played and what actually is the measure of a successful team. Inevitably, we used at first to look at people like New Zealand as the benchmark for us. I remember in the early days all the video clips that we showed the players, where we tried to illustrate what works well on a rugby field – it was all New Zealand. After four years, we had our own clips where we could say that was terrific, this was great.

We also arranged individual appraisals and counselling when we were away on training camps, away from competition.

On the debriefing of a match, can you say how you did that?

Typically the games would be on a Saturday, and I said very little immediately after the game. The winning or losing changes very little. I don't believe in saying a great deal too soon. The players know if they have played well and they know if they have played badly, and usually they are in some sort of emotional state which inhibits rational thinking. If the debrief is too soon they tend to think and say all sorts of strange things, so there is usually a gap and the sad thing was that typically for England matches, we didn't meet again until at least a week later. I think in hindsight I would have preferred perhaps a Sunday morning debriefing session in some instances, but it was never possible or practical. So we would usually meet the following weekend when we were on a fortnightly cycle of matches, which we would be typically in the Five Nations. The difficulty was they had all been playing in a club game on the Saturday prior to assembling that evening. After dinner together we would get together and just cast our minds back to the previous Saturday and ask them straight away 'What do you think, what was good, what was not so good, what are the areas do you think we've got to concentrate on?'.

What about when you were in the World Cup - how did you do it then?

In the World Cup, we would play a game, do the social niceties and stuff, whatever is advised, then go back to our hotel. We would have a half hour of immediate thoughts and then we would relax and switch off. We would set some tasks to think about before the next day. On the next day we would work with specific players to think about their particular area. We would also have the video of the game and the management, usually myself and the coach, would look at certain things and extract some short clips to illustrate points. However, we always made a point of letting the players say what they thought first and then built on that. Again, it's all part of this ownership I think, it is their responsibility, and they have to be self-analytical and self-critical. Eventually they became probably ultra-critical.

Just say a little bit more about that over-critical thing – becoming too self-critical.

Well, you sometimes become so obsessed with fine detail, you can lose the big picture. I think once or twice certain players did get too involved in minutiae and their first reaction was all the little things that went wrong. In those circumstances I had to say things such as 'Well, so what, what was the big effect of that? What about the major things, what was the major good thing? What was it that really made us win? What was it that made a difference there? What was it that caused us almost to lose?' I had to try to help them get the big picture right instead of little things. They had become obsessed with their own little technical things and you have to say 'Well, it doesn't matter too much really at the end of the day.' I just felt that one or two of the players, particularly the older players, were like that. On the other hand, the younger players were so wrapped up in the experience that they often saw too little of the detail. I even felt a little guilty when I had to focus the younger players on detail. It is trying to keep that balance, I suppose. I often found that difficult, I must admit.

Looking back on several years of outstandingly consistent success, what do you see now, retrospectively, as the qualities that the team exhibited that made it for you a really high-performing team?

I suppose the fundamental thing was that a group of pretty good players came together and developed a real shared commitment to being the best. There was a huge team bonding and our critics said we carried it too far, and judging that moment where confidence becomes complacency, I think, has always been very difficult. Some people new to the team said that as the team dynamic progressed, coming into the team at first felt uncomfortable because they felt like outsiders coming into a family. I know the present management are trying to recapture this feeling because I have seen them recently talking about 'Club England'. I used to say that they were English players who temporarily went back to their clubs, and that they had to constantly think of themselves as an England player. This was their club here, their team, their friends, the people they were going to stand shoulder to shoulder with when the flak starts, rather than club players who periodically got together to play for England.

So, how did you integrate those new ones – it sounds like a pretty critical issue?

Yes, I think it is one of the hardest things for a coach to do. If you are with a team over a period of time you know that no team is really that stable; they give an illusion of stability. When I look back we had an illusion of stability and consistency; in fact, the team changed by as many as five people each year. Now that's a third of a rugby team and yet the illusion was that the team hardly changed for four years. We coped with it easily enough because I probably still had enough freshness in me to change my words slightly to say the same things to new players without being too repetitive for the more experienced players. I was growing with the team, so for the first two or three years, integration was not really a problem. New seasons brought new challenges. The new people that were selected into the squad quickly picked up the values and behaviours. We paired them with experienced players and they quickly picked up the atmosphere of the squad. In the team discussions we were probably saying similar things, but we were moving on as well so it was exciting for everyone. After four or five years, that's when it starts to get difficult to integrate new people because you have some who have been with you all the time, the core of the team. If you can maintain your core you can manage to tinker with the periphery of the team as long as you've got the core to carry you through. But after five years, you hear yourself starting to say the same things over and over again, and you fear that those who have been there all this time have switched off because you are not saying anything new to them, and yet if you are not careful you do not remind them and the new members of all the things that were important to success in the preceding years. I found that really challenging. Eventually I think that caused me to stop more than anything else. I didn't feel I had any freshness left in me and I couldn't cope with saying to the new players what I felt had to be said, and to recognize that these three or four over here had heard all this before and were saying 'here we go again'. I did not find an easy way to cope with this.

What was the role of your captains and your senior pros in developing a team – how did you utilize them?

We used to get them together as a group periodically and chat to them. They were our trusted lieutenants. They had been through campaigns before, accumulated great experience and provided important insights into the challenges for the team in the season ahead. We would ask for their input as to what they felt we should do differently this season to last season; or, prior to a particular game, how they felt we should approach it; or, how best to integrate the new players in the squad. We used them in a wide variety of ways and then they would have to make sure that they were providing the support/reinforcement that we, the management, had been wanting. They also fed back to us any vibes that we weren't doing it right or if there was any uncertainly amongst the new younger players, people who did not understand roles, what we were trying to do. So it was very much a network. I have never been a believer in making the captain carry all the responsibility. We had a captain who earlier in his career had less experience than another half dozen players in the team. Trying to get them to really make that experience count and communicate with each on the field was very important. We did not succeed there in some ways. We didn't have many natural leaders. That always was a weakness and I think it was a major factor in the relative underachievement for the potential of the team that we developed. I still don't think that the team, even at the height of its powers, achieved as much as it should have done. We had some spectacular failures.

Generating leadership and decision-making abilities within the team was critical to our success and yet very challenging. We would explore as many 'what ifs' as we could so that the players could more easily recognize the key cues within the match and respond both individually and as a team in an appropriate manner. The players had the power to change things on the field; the work we did with them beforehand was aimed at helping them make those critical decisions as successfully as possible.

How did you sort out differences of opinion amongst the players regarding the appropriate responses to situations within the match?

Firstly, by creating situations in which players were confident to voice and discuss their opinion. This was best achieved through small group discussion on specific issues and situations. From the small group we would take the issue into a larger forum. In addition, the management would involve themselves in these discussions either with the players or as a separate group, whatever was most appropriate. The key was to generate the discussion.

What was the process for deselection of a player?

This was always a difficult step and although we had a squad system that made things a little easier, it was always challenging. Generally the process followed the following pattern: discussion within the management team; discussion with captain; sleep on the decision and review/confirm next day; talk to the player, preferably face to face; allow the player time to reflect before detailed discussion on their way forward.

In this way we tried to put the player at the centre of the process and understand their needs even though it was a relatively negative experience for them.

What was the pattern of meetings prior to major matches?

The pre-match procedures were drawn together in consultation with the players, and while they varied according to the specific situations the general pattern for something like the Five Nations Championship was as follows:

- Wednesday. Team meet in the afternoon and have practice session. Preliminary meetings in the evening.
- Thursday. Briefing meetings in the morning regarding opponents followed by a practice session that was closed to media. Press conference later in the day. Evening team meeting to highlight key areas of attention for this match.
- Friday. Management team steps back to allow captain and players to take greater responsibility for final run-in to the match. Rest and relaxation plus team meeting in the evening (led by captain). Motivational video generating positive image provided by management/support team.
- Saturday, Match Day. 'Unit' meetings run by key players in mid-morning. Planned food and fluid intake. Short meeting at lunchtime to focus attention (video and a few words from management). Arrive at ground seventy-five minutes prior to kick-off. Opportunity for management to talk individually to players. Final forty-five minutes is a combination of individuals going through their personal preparations and drawing the team or units together for group preparation. The details and timings of this are decided with the captain.

What have been the key learning points that you would offer to an aspiring club coach?

- Give quality time to talking to players to generate real understanding of the critical factors that lead to success.
- Be methodical and give real attention to detail. Preparation is the key to high performance.
- Rigorously prioritize the use of your limited time with performers.
- Generate real understanding in the players regarding what is happening on the pitch in all aspects of their play, both individually and as a team.
- Plan strategically over the longer term leading up to major competitions. It is important to provide the bigger picture for performers (e.g. over time) so they can plan their performance development with the most appropriate goal in mind.

- A small, highly focussed management team has distinct advantages for both the management and the players.

England and Great Britain Hockey, 1983–96

The second case study is with Sue Slocombe OBE, who worked with senior international teams in women's hockey from 1983 to 1996. During this time Sue was one of the very few female coaches working at this level. She led the England senior team to silver and gold medals at European Championships in 1987 and 1991 respectively. In 1993 she began work with the Great Britain Olympic Squad, taking them through to the Atlanta Olympics where they narrowly missed the bronze medal in a play-off against the Netherlands. Sue was one of the first coaches to integrate the whole range of the sports sciences into her work with players at both club and international level. In all her work she has followed her fundamental belief that the players should be deeply involved in their own learning and in the latter years extended this principle into areas of team development that previous coaches in team sports had feared to tread. She was UK Coach of the Year in 1991.

What was your role as the coach in the development of the hockey team during the 1980s and 1990s?

I suppose my role changed over time in the 1980s. I was in a management team where the coach's role focused on the technical and tactical aspects of the development of the team. I viewed the role in a much more holistic way which included the management of all areas of development of the performer. I still believe that is the right approach a coach should have, rather then only concentrating on the technical and tactical aspects. By the start of the Olympic cycle, it had been decided by the Great Britain Board that the management team should be coach-led. This was the first time that had happened and so my role then included integrating a management team working together. This team included sports scientists, coaches, medical staff and management support.

How did you manage that transition?

It was a slow transition. The person who was appointed as manager had been a coach herself and valued the way that I was trying to develop my work with players. This made the transition easier in that the philosophy was one that had both of our support. In the early stages, there were some players and people in the sport who wondered why I was putting such a high focus on areas other than just the technical and tactical. I guess in some ways my thinking was ahead of people around me, because if you look at what is happening within elite performance now, the holistic approach is the one that top sports are adopting. To help me achieve the transition I just gradually extended my own understanding of areas that I was not very strong in; I just went out and learnt. I learnt from others who knew more than I did.

How did you decide on the boundaries of your roles with the manager such that you could follow the holistic approach and yet get the right balance in your roles?

That's easy to answer. We sat down and talked about it. We looked at what we thought were responsibilities that needed to be addressed to ensure that it was an effective programme for players, and then who was to carry it out. The players needed to know who was responsible for what and we wanted to involve them in decision-making. We identified what needed to be done and who was in the best position to do it. We wrote this down, including roles and responsibilities of all members of the management and support team. Where there were areas we weren't sure about, we came up with an agreement of who was responsible for what. We then shared this with our players. We even got them to say what they thought we did, to see how it matched with what we thought. In this way we fine tuned our roles accordingly. Everyone knew their roles and players were clear about our roles.

That sounds like everything in the management team was rosy and easily resolved. How did you deal with differences of opinion within the management team?

First of all, it was not all rosy. We were working under the constraint that none of us was full time and therefore communication was not as effective as it might have been. In retrospect, we needed more opportunity for the management team to sit down and talk about what was happening to ensure everybody knew the things they needed to know, and also had the opportunity to voice their own opinions. We did not have that opportunity often enough, because the management team had full time jobs elsewhere. So one of the keys to 'Team Spirit' is getting people together and talking and sharing ideas. With regard to areas of conflict and misunderstanding, the way we dealt with something like that was to sit down and talk. As it was a coach-led management team, ultimately I was responsible and there were some very difficult decisions I had to make which did conflict with members of the management team.

You mentioned about the support management team not being able to always be there with the same degree of commitment in time as the manager and the coach. How did you establish their role in the develop-

ment of the team, and what was the role of the support team/management team in the development of your players?

In the early stages there were only three in our management team, the coach, manager and physio, making it relatively easy to discuss roles and responsibility. As we increased the personnel, it became increasingly difficult as we worked on a voluntary basis. Latterly we prioritized time to discuss our roles so everyone contributed to clarifying what their role was in the development of the team. In broad terms the doctor and physio managed injury prevention, injury and illness treatment and rehabilitation. The match analyst videoed matches, edited tapes, produced motivation tapes, and generally took responsibility for anything to do with video work. The assistant coach worked closely with me and any other support coaches, specialist coaches on the technical and tactical developments, while the manager oversaw the travel, accommodation and so on. My role included overviewing the work of the sports scientists, the physiologist, psychologist and nutritionist, and integrating their input into the overall programme. However, this makes it all sound straightforward whereas in reality roles and responsibilities are much more complex than this. Often they overlap, and it is how this overlap is managed that is critical, and we did this through talking. If one member of the team was overworked then someone else would step in and help even when it was outside their role. Supporting each other in this way was critical.

What were the qualities you found your high-performing team exhibiting?

Key qualities that I found my high-performing teams exhibiting included taking responsibility over a range of issues including their own personal development, and the ability to set individual and team goals; the ability to contribute to decision-making, to reflect on their own play and to take responsibility for outcomes.

Players have an awful lot of knowledge themselves. When I had been a player, I felt I had a lot of knowledge which was rarely drawn upon. So when I was coaching, I wanted to involve the players in decision-making. Sometimes a player can be very selfish and see things which are only closely related to themselves, while the coach has an overview. The coach's role is to pull all of that together to make a team. I looked to tap into this wealth of knowledge through lots of discussion. Large and small group discussions, individual conferencing sessions with players, players discussing critical issues without members of the management team present and then deciding how they would feed back. Players helping to look at the opposition and coming up with ways that they think we should play. Of course in the end as coach I had to take responsibility and make the final decisions.

This process that you went through to actually tap into this knowledge and experience, what did you find that caused to happen in the team? What did you then find when the team performed really well as a result of this and won the European Gold Medal? What did you see that team exhibiting now that it hadn't been exhibiting in the past?

Initially some of the players showed a touch of fear. This was a phase they went through when I started to involve them. Some players were very reluctant to get involved in the decision-making. Some felt that the coach should be the fount of all knowledge, as they had always had that experience in that many coaches present themselves that way. Others may have felt I was testing them when I was asking them questions, and if they got it wrong, then I would perhaps have deselected them for the next stage. Of course it was none of that. There was a process that we went through where they actually began to realize that I did value what they had to say, and it wasn't going to affect selection. By the time we played in the European Cup in 1991, I saw a team with everyone playing for the team and not for themselves. You need individuals, but what we had in the European Cup when we won the gold medal, was the most powerful team with whom I had ever been involved. I had been involved since 1983, so it had been a long, slow process developing the players to work in that way, to be empowered to make decisions themselves, and to be involved in the decision-making. The second time I saw this was in the Atlanta Olympics in 1996. I think a lot of people didn't even expect us to qualify and although as individuals the players were not as strong as some of the other teams, we managed to achieve fourth place in the Olympics, only narrowly missing out on the bronze medal, losing on penalty strokes. I believe that our way of working had developed a very strong team performance.

The common theme in both those teams seems to be this enormous strength of the team at the end of this process. Looking back on it, how much did the need for this very strong team actually affect selection of the players?

Well, it certainly didn't mean that if somebody was a bit of an awkward customer, I didn't select them. Within both those squads there were definitely individuals who frustrated some of the other players because they were sometimes very self-centered, particularly players who were battling for their positions. To promote team working, I included a lot of work focusing on group dynamics. The players probably didn't even recognize what was happening when I carefully grouped players in discussion groups. If there were two players who really didn't get on well, then very often they were put together in a group to discuss things. What we saw evolve was that they began to work more effectively together. Out on the pitch there would be times when I would go to a group who were working on some aspect of unit play, and used questions encouraging them to work together and come up with ideas as a group. I encouraged players to try and view things from the others' point of view. We worked practically in groups, sometimes the strikers would work together, the mid-field, the defence, the strikers, so that they were working with people who were actually challenging them for places in the final selection. There was no doubt that by working together, talking together, sharing ideas, I saw twenty-four players who were actually working towards a common goal.

What were the key selection criteria that you found were essential in your mind?

I had to look at what kind of team we were trying to build, how we were going to play and the balance we needed within the sixteen players. We were trying to play a flexible game so the players had to be able to attack and defend, and that was one of our main criteria. Another selection criteria was based upon level of fitness needed to sustain our style of hockey. I was also looking for players who had mental toughness. I learnt a long time ago that the player with the most flair in training may not be the most effective under pressure of international matches. Some players with great flair crumble under pressure while others who don't stand out in training or practice matches handled the pressure of important international matches far better. Obviously there also has to be a high level of technical ability and tactical awareness.

OK, so you had a set of criteria, the players were part of developing that criteria and therefore by definition the players knew what they had to do in order to succeed. In the two experiences you have mentioned of creating high-quality teams at world level, how important is continuity of personnel?

Continuity is important. However, you just don't keep somebody in for the sake of continuity, it is a little bit more complex than that. There's no doubt that you need time to be able to develop players into working in a team. It just doesn't happen rapidly. In the early days we weren't together very much, and developing a team took even longer, as there would be several weeks between training sessions. In time we educated the players to prepare themselves for a training weekend so they could start from close to where we left off at the previous training in order to really move things forward. We had a large training squad so we did have the opportunity for continuity, but I also had to make tough decisions in that we couldn't just keep a player in the training squad for the sake of continuity. There comes a time when if a player is not making the progress they should be making, then we would have to bring in someone new. It was critical how we integrated that new player into the training squad, and how we moved the other player out.

So, how did you deselect a player – what was the process?

First of all we gave the player a long time within the group. I remember when I first got involved in coaching at international level, a player was invited in for a weekend and if they didn't perform well, they weren't in again. I thought that was terrible. You have to give players a reasonable amount of time to allow them to find their feet, to get to know people, and to become part of that group. They need to be very aware of what your expectations are of them and have expectations of themselves as well, and that requires a lot of talking. I spent a lot of time either writing to or talking with players if things weren't going quite as they should do, to give them a chance to know what it was they needed to do to improve their performance. Often they would identify the issues themselves, and together we would draw up an action plan of what they were going to do to try and improve. If they still didn't improve, then I would always be the one who was responsible for telling the player. It was probably the worst part of the job. I would always give the player reasons. That wasn't always easy, because it might be that they have played the best they possibly can but someone else is just that bit better. I would communicate the reason and what they needed to work on in the future to put them back into contention.

You mentioned also about bringing in new players. How did you integrate new players into the squad?

The basic principles were to encourage senior members of the squad to help a new player. In particular the captain and vice-captain and other senior players were very important both in training sessions on the pitch and in group discussions. I would make sure that the new player or players were with senior players that I knew would be sympathetic and empathic towards a new player. When I became Great Britain coach, I went away on a training camp for two weeks with some of the players from Scotland and Wales who had not had the same basic programme as the more experienced England players, to try and give them an opportunity to start on a level plain. We could never truly make it an even playing field, but I felt is was important to be fair to them and to try and share the experiences that perhaps other players had had.

What was the role of the captain and senior players in the development of the team?

While we tried to value every player's contribution the captain and senior players had a very key role in sharing their knowledge and experience. If, for example, there were four groups working, I would put four senior players to lead those groups and initially they would also be the ones that reported back. Then I would encourage those senior players to see whether they could get other people within their group to report back so gradually it wasn't just the senior players taking a lead. Actually, it was like a hidden curriculum, there was personal development of other players in the group being able to speak out and feed back. This was an important role of the senior players. In the latter part the captain was a defender and the vice-captain was a midfield player, so I included the most experienced striker to talk about issues. The leadership roles of the captain and vice-captain were discussed and agreed by both players and management. They were sounding boards for the players. If the players had something they wanted to voice, they could go to any member of the management team, but they would sometimes go to the captain or vice-captain, who would then pass on whatever they felt was necessary.

How do you respond to coaches, who are worried that if we empower players to the point that perhaps they have views on selection and the way the team is going, that those players will not be able to speak objectively, but hold onto their friendship patterns and personal preferences within the team itself?

Sometimes I think we underestimate just how important winning is to a team and I know from personal experience where senior players have actually said not to select a player that is a particular friend of theirs and it really surprised me the first time it happened. Winning was the most important factor to the player, not friendship. So I think the majority of the time, they are able to stand back. If they're not, when you know your players well enough you are able to recognize this, and are able to explore this with the player. As coach you can challenge a senior player, and say 'Hang on a minute – tell me why you think that player should be in the squad. Sell me the idea why that player should be in this squad.' You'll soon know partly by their body language, partly by the things they say, whether they genuinely believe that player should be in the squad and actually they might be right and you might not be right. It just needs very careful listening and exploring of issues.

This conversation makes it sound like the coach of elite performers nowadays has to develop abilities well beyond the tactical and the technical – is that your experience of nearly two decades in elite performance?

I have always thought you've got to have skills beyond the tactical and technical, and I am a little disappointed that there is still an image that the coach is the fount of all knowledge on the tactical and technical. I think the coach needs many more skills including good listening skills, communication skills and other skills way beyond just knowing their sport. It's about understanding coaching, not just knowing your sport.

Do you see in British sport those skills and abilities being developed in our coaches of elite performers?

I am sorry to say no. We are getting a better understanding of the holistic approach for players so that they are experiencing more effective programmes, but I would also like to see a more holistic approach to the development of coaches. Of course a coach needs to know their own sport, but you don't have to know everything and be the fount of all knowledge. I think the emphasis is too much upon knowledge and insufficient on understanding about the coaching process. I wonder how many coaches understand that different people learn in different ways. If I give you an example of one of my players who I did some individual work with. She was frustrated with being in the wrong place when we were trying to do a zonal defence. It just needed one person out of place and we were in trouble. When on tour we took time to go through a video and explored the situation on a flip chart. Her preferred learning style was through the visual, and she commented on how helpful this process had been. How often do coaches actually stop and think about learning preferences within their group, and therefore focus on working in that way with particular players? I believe in Britain we need to educate our elite coaches much more in learning about how people learn.

Just moving on if we can towards the tournament situations where if you speak to performers they say 'Well, we eat, we sleep and we meet and we play' and that's their life. So meetings are the bedrock of tournament play insomuch as we spend a lot of time involving ourselves with players in meetings – could you just describe some of the uses you made of meetings. Most people will think you just have a meeting before you play, and so it's just about the tactical and technical, was that your experience, is that how you used them, and if it was more than that, what were the uses of them?

Meetings are very much more important that just a briefing meeting for a match. I believe you need to be careful of having too many meetings. You need to identify the purpose of each meeting and who should attend. You don't need everybody at every meeting. There are lots of different kinds of meetings. Management meetings are critical, even if they are only short ten minute ones over dinner, when the management sits together and just reviews what's happened during the day and looks at any critical issues that have come up. I had a meeting with the medical staff before selection was done to make sure that I knew which players were fit for selection. I had short meetings with the attacking penalty corner group looking at a video of the way the opposition defended penalty corners. The players would explore possible corners that could be effective against the way the team was defending. Of course in the end as the coach I had to make the final decisions, but their input was critical. We had a meeting before finalizing the starting line-up for the next match with the captain and vice-captain to hear their views. Following this meeting I would meet with the assistant coach and manager to finalize the starting line-up. I had critical one-to-one meetings with players. A player might have underperformed and needed a bit of a boost. The manager or I always tried to speak with players who had not been selected in a starting line-up, or I had not subbed on during a match. There might be some conflict between a few players and I would sit and discuss these issues with the small group. We had a briefing meeting to discuss the game plan. We always used motivating tapes which were absolutely terrific. If you asked the players about these motivating tapes they thought of this as a highlight and felt they helped them prepare positively for the match. There was the final team meeting in the changing room when I would emphasize the key points for the match before the players went out on the pitch. There was also the half-time meeting, and then at some relevant time after a match we had a debriefing meeting. The timing of this debriefing meeting was absolutely critical. Preferably it needed to be fairly close to the match so key issues could be raised, but not so close that the emotions were still running high and players found it hard to reflect effectively. So there are all kinds of different meeting and I have mentioned some we had. However, it is important to clarify the purpose and who should attend, and keep it short and sharp and to the point.

Could you just take us through the timetable of an international match, two o'clock in the afternoon, just very slickly: what would happen in the day, what would be the timetable that those players, in consultation with the management team, had agreed would be the best for them, and let's assume that you have a, let's say, 15–30 minute drive to the stadium.

The principles behind the timing and content of the daily programme were discussed and agreed by players and management well before the tournament. The details were then agreed by the management and posted the day before.

   We would work back from the match time, so a run and mobility would be before an 8.0–8.30 breakfast. Following breakfast there was a time for players to see the physio and/or doctor. Eleven o'clock would be the match briefing meeting then a stop for food at 12 noon. There was then a period of relaxation when players had to be in their rooms and find their own way of relaxing and focusing on the game plan. How they chose to relax had been explored and agreed well before the tournament.

Throughout the morning players would be topping up with fluid. We aimed to arrive at the ground about one hour before the start of the match. They would go out and do their warm-up as a team. The warm-up was designed with the players. They identified what they wanted to do, with some team parts and some individual parts. Each squad I've worked with has come up with a different pre-match. We would then return to the changing rooms for a brief meeting focusing on key points and team building. We always sang the national anthem if it was not going to be played on the pitch, as a group in a very close tight unit and then we went out for the match.

How were the matches debriefed – what was the process, what went on after the game that led to, in your experience, high-quality debriefing of matches?

The timing is critical as is the debriefing process. I learnt a very painful experience at a major tournament about debriefing. We lost a game that we shouldn't have lost. We scored two goals which should have been allowed but we lost 1-0. We managed the debrief poorly by focusing too heavily on the loss as opposed to addressing a few key points then moving onto the game plan for the next match.

I had consulted the captain, vice-captain and management team and we agreed a process, but I had a gut feeling that it was not the right thing, and it wasn't. The next time I found myself in a similar situation in the Olympic Qualifier, I used my intuition and this proved more effective. I managed the debrief totally differently, focusing on a few key learning points then moving on to thinking about the next game. Players reflected back after the tournament that this had been a key factor in building confidence in the squad. A similar situation happened in Atlanta when we again lost the first match, albeit to a team that was considered much stronger than us. Again I followed my intuition which on reflection was a good decision. It is very important not to dwell on what's just happened, whether you have won or lost, but actually to get some key points from it and move on.

In a debrief the players did the talking to start with, working in small groups then feeding back key issues to the whole squad. There were either four groups, led by a senior player, or three groups, the defence, midfield and strikers. Sometimes they worked in small groups of playing units. They had a short time discussing, reflecting back on the goals they had set and the game plan, and identifying what areas needed to be considered to help us in the next game. When they had all contributed, then I would add any additional thoughts. The players usually came up with 80–90 per cent of the things that I would have said. It didn't need me to stand there and tell them what they had done well and hadn't done well. They know these things. It's just a few details that sometimes they don't spot. Using questions often drew out further key issues. Involving the players in the debrief created a positive environment, with them taking responsibility for the match and then suggesting areas for further development for the next match.

I am hearing that there was a lot of conversation and reflection by the players themselves, so how did the use of video come in during tournaments?

Video is a very powerful tool as the evidence is there for us all to see. Over the years I refined the way I used video. Some players are uncomfortable seeing themselves making mistakes. I found I needed to be careful how I used video. However, sometimes you have to go through a painful process for players to acknowledge what really happened. I looked at video much more than the players. Our match analyst did a terrific job editing for me. I would say what I wanted, giving him as much time to produce the edited video as possible. Where I considered it would be beneficial for players to see any edits, then I would organize a meeting. Often players asked if they could see videos and I set aside an extra video recorder for them to be able to view what they wanted in their free time. I used edited videos showing how a team defended penalties and our attacking penalty corner group would look at this and offer suggestions of which of our corners would be effective. I had already seen the video and made my own decisions, but by asking the players they were involved in the decision-making about which corners we might use. I went through a similar process looking at edited videos of opposition attacking penalty corners and our defending group considering the most effective way to defend. I did this with a number of key areas regarding tactics, and again players were involved in the decision-making. As coach I took responsibility for the final decisions. We also used edited videos to look closely at key players in the opposition, identifying their strengths and weaknesses.

As already mentioned, we also used video as a motivating tool.

Just looking at various types of competitions that teams go into, what are the key differences for you as a coach between the single matches that international teams play versus the tournaments that they play versus perhaps even tours that they may go on rather than tournaments?

Yes, there are critical differences. Unfortunately the press and some of our own supporters sometimes don't understand why we play certain teams in certain matches, and why we don't always put out our best side. What if your key penalty corner striker is injured in the Olympics? You need to have players that can cover all eventualities. I would look at 'what ifs' and consider these during the build-up to a tournament. If you have never played a game without using other people and you lose a key player in the Olympics, what are you going to do?

If I look at individual matches first. It depended on which phase of development we were in. In the early phases I would use matches to see how other players coped with pressure situations to help with selection. The further away it was from the tournament, the more the focus was on giving different people experience, how they played together, trying different units on the pitch to see which played well as a team on the right and so on. The nearer I got to a tournament, the more likely I was to be playing my strongest group because we were practising for the tournament, and this was progressing towards a consolidation phase and fine tuning.

The key issues surrounding tournaments that were not major tournaments were similar to those for individual matches. I would use a tournament like individual matches, depending on how far they were from the major tournament we were building towards. For a major tournament my goal was for us to perform to our maximum potential, so my selection was based on picking the starting line-up and making substitutions to achieve the best result we could.

Tours provided a time for development in identified areas including further education in non-sport-specific areas. They were also opportunities to see how people coped away from home and living with the squad. There was usually more time for talking as we were living together for a longer period than usual. I focused a great deal on team-building activities during tours, both in building the management as a team and the players.

In these major tournaments, what was your role and what did you do when things were going badly with the team?

My role obviously included preparation for matches, finalizing game plans etc. In addition I considered my role to be supporting the players so they could achieve their maximum potential. This can be a challenging role when things aren't going so well. I found this extremely difficult in one World Cup. I hardly slept at all, because even the experienced players were putting more and more demands on me. I was trying to support the less experienced players and with less than twenty-four hours between some matches, trying to debrief the match, look at the videos, prepare for the next match, eat, sleep and support the players, there wasn't sufficient time to do all this well. I tried to identify those players I thought needed extra support and spoke with them, and would be available for others to come to me should they so choose. When debriefing the tournament, some senior players identified that they would have liked more of my time during the pressure periods. When I shared with them the impossibility of what was being expected of me, we looked at ways that, should we go through a difficult period again, we might manage this more effectively. This included players taking even more responsibility themselves.

Developing towards this was a major issue during the next phase towards the Olympic Qualifier. Some people may consider this to be developing mental toughness. My gut reaction is that we developed a squad for the next two major tournaments who were mentally much tougher and our results indicate that we were more successful, moving from ninth in the world in 1994 to fourth at the Atlanta Olympics.

What was the role of the rest of the management team when things were going badly?

In theory all members of the management had a role in supporting players. However, some people are more comfortable addressing critical issues when the going gets tough, while others find these situations difficult to manage. The manager I was fortunate enough to work with, Jenny Cardwell, was terrific. She was excellent in supporting the players and trying to find ways forward. We identified ways before a major tournament of how we would manage difficult times. For example, who would be responsible for speaking with which players, who would speak to those who were not in a starting line-up. We talked daily about any concerns and who would deal with them. We also gave personal support to each other when the going got tough. We were a little like the geese flying in formation. When one of us was flagging a little the other one stepped in to relieve the pressure. I felt we worked in a real partnership, creating support to the players so they could achieve their maximum potential. The physio's room was a safe place where players often went to chat and share ideas. It became like the counsellor's room. We all really had a key role. Sometimes it became absolutely draining. Sometimes I think this is a gender issue, as my experience of coaching women is that women need a lot of support there. They also had their own support. They talked to each other and supported each other. The captain and vice-captain also had a critical role in supporting players when things weren't going well.

Could you just reflect on one instance where things were going badly and you did some things and it turned it round?

When we were in Atlanta we lost the first game 5-0 to Korea. I remember being interviewed as I was walking off the pitch. I was so positive and was parking that game. Prior to the Olympics one of my personal 'What ifs' had been how I would manage the situation if we lost the first match. I'd anticipated that we were likely to lose to Korea as I rated them as one of the top two teams in the world. Of course you want to win every game, but as coach you must also be realistic and have realistic goals. We did not have a squad that was likely to win the gold or silver. I had also decided the importance of remaining positive as it was only the first match in the tournament. I remained very positive and helped the players debrief the match, identifying two very key issues which had contributed to our defeat and then we focused on the next match. I think this was a major turning point. Players commented to me at a later stage that this had been a critical point in the Olympics and my positive approach had helped them manage the loss against Korea.

As you now reflect on probably many years at the sharp end of international sport, what have been your greatest learning points regarding the development of high-performing teams?

Commitment from the coach is critical. Commitment, and dedication and focus from players and management. Recognizing that it takes time to build a high-performing team. There will be highs and lows, and learning how to come through those lows and learn from the experiences is important. Someone once said 'the secret of success is managing the failures', and I believe this is critical. Time for both the management team and players to develop working as a team is also critical. One of my disappointments was that I was never in a position to be really able to develop the management working really effectively as a high performing team, as they were not full-time. Considering that all of us had jobs elsewhere we didn't do so badly! To develop a high-performing team it is important to listen to what people have got to say and to value other's views. Empowering and involving players in decision-making, helping them to take responsibility is critical, while following your intuition is also critical. Detailed planning and preparation with attention to detail is fundamental.

What would you offer as some of your key experiences for the benefit of coaches who at club level are seeking to develop their team, such that they can be even more successful?

Things I mentioned in answer to your last question would be things I would say to a club coach. Although, having been a club coach myself, time is a critical issue in that you are having to prepare your squad almost on a weekly basis to win matches. I would add that I know we can all learn from each other. I would encourage club coaches to listen to what other people say, to be open-minded but in the end to do it their way. You have to find your own way of doing things. Just be yourself. Don't think you always know everything, don't be frightened to admit that you might have learnt something from somebody else. Think in a holistic way, think about the players you are coaching. I believe that as coaches we have a responsibility for the personal development of the players we work with, no matter what their age and ability.

Bibliography

Hemery, D., *Sporting Excellence* (Collins Willow, 1991)

Katzenbach, J. and Smith, D., *The Wisdom of Teams* (Harvard Business School Press, 1993)

Whitaker, D., *Coaching Workshop* (The Crowood Press, 1992)

Whitmore, J., *Coaching for Performance* (Nicholas Brearley Publishing Ltd., 1996)

Index